D-DAY
DECODED

'Les dés sont sur le tapis'
(The die is cast)

Coded BBC message to the Resistance in Caen
to prepare for an imminent attack

Acknowledgements

Researched and written by William Jordan;
the author has asserted his moral rights.
Edited by Simon Thraves and Gill Knappett.
Designed by Katie Beard.
Front cover design by Katie Beard.
Map by Glad Stockdale.

Illustrations reproduced by kind permission of
Getty Images and the Imperial War Museum.

Quotes on pages 10, 17, 33 and 58 are reproduced by kind
permission of Curtis Brown Ltd, London, on behalf of
The Estate of Winston Churchill © Winston S. Churchill.

Available through mail order. See our website,
www.pitkin-guides.com, for our full range of titles,
or contact us for a copy of our brochure.

Pitkin Publishing, Healey House, Dene Road,
Andover, Hampshire SP10 2AA, UK
Sales and enquiries: 01264 409200
Fax: 01264 334110
Email: sales@thehistorypress.co.uk

Printed in India.
ISBN: 978-1-84165-348-8   2/12

CONTENTS

N.B. All dates in the text refer to 1944 unless otherwise indicated. Measurements of weight and distance are given in Imperial for the Allies and in metric for the opposition – in keeping with the period.

INTRODUCTION

From condoms to corundum paste, inflatable belts to inflatable tanks, the Allies appear to have thought of everything. A single copy of the Overlord Plan with appendices weighed in at 36lb of paper and filled a filing cabinet. Operation NEPTUNE covered 900 pages of typed foolscap. Nothing would be left to chance – except the weather. The biggest amphibious operation of all time involved millions, but its secret held good after two postponements, to daybreak, Tuesday 6 June 1944.

No German *techniker* (*Funkmeßgerätetechniker*, radar operator), sailor, soldier or spy was able to raise the general alarm in advance of that moment. The Luftwaffe was grounded by the poor weather. Rommel was 800km away for his wife's birthday party. A third of his senior officers in Normandy were playing war games in Brittany, and had a football match planned for the 6th. In the evening of the 5th, his Chief of Staff was dining with the anti-Hitler conspirators of the *Schwarzekappelle*, the Black Orchestra. In Paris, Rommel's boss Field Marshal Gerd Von Rundstedt was at dinner with his son, and sceptical about this latest fuss: it had to be another British trick, announcing the imminence of the invasion after the BBC evening news! As for Hitler himself, he was going to make an effort to get up early in order to meet the Hungarian Prime Minister.

So, if you have ever asked yourself:

- What does the 'D' in D-Day mean?
- Just how was the greatest secret of the war – the time and place of the operation – maintained?
- Why were the Landing Beaches named Utah, Omaha, Gold, Juno and Sword?
- How were two harbours the size of Dover manufactured, assembled and towed across the English Channel without being attacked, or even noticed?
- Who, before D-Day, unwittingly revealed the key code names to the world?
- Which valiant bird won a D-Day medal?
- What did the Brick, the Duck and an enigmatic 30ft-diameter steel Cotton Reel with the weight of a destroyer have in common?
- Who was it that created a Rhino by chopping up Hedgehogs – and why?
- What were the roles of Pluto, Bimbo and Bambi in fuelling the liberation of Disney's ancestral home?
- And what have sobbing violins got to do with it?

The answers lurk in this little book.

'Much the greatest thing that we have ever attempted.'
(Winston Churchill on Overlord)

The first letters of the alphabet help recall the complicated sequence of attacks carried out by the US Airborne missions into the Cherbourg peninsula. A total of 13,348 men were brought in over the western seaboard, 13,100 dropped in six Drop Zones, three per division. One man in five was a casualty, one in five in the right place by the end of the day. Missions <u>A</u>LBANY and <u>B</u>OSTON crossed at 500 feet in 821 Dakotas in serials 1,000 feet apart, nine aircraft in each forming 'Vee-in-Vee's' (three sub-serials forming V-shapes within the V of nine). Nine of the 20 serials hit heavy cloud. Two hours later, in <u>C</u>HICAGO and <u>D</u>ETROIT, 104 Waco gliders were towed in over the 'hedgerow country', bearing 375 men, artillery, jeeps and medics at a cost of 81 casualties. From 2100 hours <u>E</u>LMIRA (157 casualties) and <u>K</u>EOKUCK (none) consisted of 208 Horsas and 36 Wacos; <u>G</u>ALVESTON (117) and <u>H</u>ACKENSTACK (75), 154 Horsas and 50 Wacos, brought in another thousand men, 20 guns and 40 vehicles from 0655 on 7 June. The daylight missions were closely escorted by Allied fighters, and the last glider landing was about 1015.

A definitive analysis of US D-Day Airborne casualties can be consulted on http://www.6juin1944.com/assaut/aeropus/en_page.php?page =statistics. The mission lasted 33 days.

ABLE BAKER, JNCLE VICTOR

Only short sections of each beach sector were used for landings. The sub-sections were based upon a US Army/Navy radio phonetic alphabet developed in 1941. It was easy to pronounce and hear over the airwaves. In 1943 the plan, reading from west to east, was without beach names, but the sub-divisions were in place: ABLE BAKER CHARLIE <u>DOG</u> <u>EASY</u> <u>FOX</u> – GEORGE HOWE <u>ITEM</u> <u>KING</u> LOVE – <u>MIKE</u> <u>NAN</u> – OBOE PETER <u>QUEEN</u> <u>ROGER</u>. When the beachhead plan was extended west in 1944 it also included SUGAR <u>TARE</u> <u>UNCLE</u> VICTOR WILLIAM – Utah Beach.

The underlined code words were used for beach landings. The colours GREEN WHITE and RED allowed for further precision in planning: DOG GREEN, the worst place to land at H-Hour (0630+), was 1,000 yards long. Separating the British from the Americans at H-Hour were 10 miles of cliffs and reefs (GEORGE HOWE), and no attempt was made to attack these sectors by sea.

In May 1944 German communication lines and the building programme for the Atlantic Wall were disrupted by the 'Transportation Plan'. Instead of bombing Germany, Allied Air Forces gave priority to France's communications networks. 76,000 tons of bombs were dropped on 80 rail centres, while the strafing of trains began on 20 May. However, in 200,000 sorties, 12,000 Allied airmen in 1,953 aircraft were shot down in April and May, 85 per cent from 'ack-ack'(anti-aircraft gunfire). On 30 May all the bridges over the Seine were destroyed. There were also 2,500 sorties against coastal batteries.

The Luftwaffe was losing its experienced pilots faster than it could produce aircraft to replace the losses. On D-Day its fighters made only 70 sorties, just two in daylight over the beaches, with only 319 aircraft of all types, against 14,674 Allied sorties by 11,590 aeroplanes crewed by around 70,000 men.

Landing on Gold Beach, Private Mullaly, responding to CSM Hollis's observation of a row of birds sitting quietly on the barbed wire in front of them, said, 'No bloody wonder, Sarge, there's no bloody room for them in the air.'

AQUATINT

Eleven British commandos, in a 'Small Scale Raiding Force' led by Major Gustavus March-Phillips, landed on the future Omaha Beach (later DOG WHITE) on the night of 12/13 September 1942 to glean information about the beach and capture some guards. The group included an English Peer of the Realm, a Free French Naval officer, a Polish Jew and a German Communist. They were almost all killed on the spot when they set off a guard dog after floundering in the pitch dark for 50 minutes, but one of them, Captain Graham Hayes MC, 29, survived, only to be betrayed in France and executed on 13 July 1943 [3:71 Viroflay Cemetery]. March-Phillips, 34, Private Richard Lehniger, 42, and Sergeant Alan Williams, 22, are buried in Saint Laurent Cemetery (Omaha). Lehinger's CWGC gravestone reads: '*Die International wird die menschheit sein.*' ('The Internationale shall become humanity.')

Failed commando raids, together with Dieppe, provided Goebbels with valuable propaganda to pronounce to the world the futility of attempting a landing.

Source: *Aquatint*, André Heintz and Gérard Fournier (OREP);
CWGC (Commonwealth War Grave Commission): the words '*Die International wird die menschheit sein* are from the *International* (the anthem of international socialism, the de facto hymn of the USSR)

ASPARAGUS

Stripped tree trunks were set up as anti-glider poles in the fields. They would also have featured fused shells and grenades suspended from interconnecting wires. By 9 May, 170,000 had been installed in the Cherbourg peninsula alone. Like the mine-laying programme, it was far from finished come D-Day. The poles could even help a glider make a landing by slowing it down before it slammed into something else – like a wall. They hindered the night-time attack very little: casualties were more likely to be caused by hedges, trees, telephone poles and buildings. Rommel's 'asparagus' were then destroyed for the daylight attacks that followed. After D-Day it was reported that some of the freed Italians, press-ganged by the Germans to erect the poles, resumed the task for want of anything else to do!

De Gaulle was kept out of the picture until 4 June, when Churchill summoned him from Algiers, laying on his personal plane. After Eisenhower's own speech at 1100 hours, the King of Norway, the Prime Minister of Belgium, the Grand Duchess of Luxembourg and the Queen of the Netherlands broadcast speeches prepared by SHAEF (Supreme Headquarters Allied Expeditionary Force) to their peoples. De Gaulle refused to do so (though he was not even a Head of State) but was finally allowed to broadcast a speech of his own devising in the evening. It proved to be a magnificent rallying call – which the BBC omitted to record.

'Derrière le nuage si lourd de notre sang et de nos larmes, voici que reparaît le soleil de notre grandeur ....' ('Behind the cloud heavy with our blood and our tears, here again appears the sunlight of our grandeur ....')

The speech risked sparking civil war. German reprisals led to a futile attempt by SHAEF to cancel this general call to arms on 10 June.

De Gaulle was given his own codes but, despite assurances to the contrary, there was close British surveillance of all his messages and movements.

BAGRATION

As the Western Allies prepared nine divisions to confront seven German divisions in France, Stalin ('Uncle Joe') was preparing 165 divisions to eject the Germans from the USSR. Stalin faced 228 German divisions, over 2 million men. Bagration was the name of the Georgian military hero who had fought against Napoleon, and the campaign was launched on 22 June 1944, three years to the day after the German invasion (BARBAROSSA). A total of 17 German divisions were completely destroyed, another 50 took losses of over 50 per cent; the final German losses would total 1.5 million. The campaigns in the East were characterized by ruthlessness and cruelty on both sides.

D-Day was but one part of a vast pincer movement closing in on Hitler's Reich. Despite the vast Soviet sacrifice, on 1 April 1944 Churchill wrote, 'Although I have tried in every way to put myself in sympathy with these Communist leaders, I cannot feel the slightest trust or confidence in them. Force and facts are their only realities.' Indeed, Lenin had once remarked of Stalin, 'Beware of Comrade Stalin, he is the new Genghis Khan, he will slaughter us all.'

After Dunkirk the BBC appealed for postcards of France to help map the coast for the return trip and over 10 million were eventually collected. De Gaulle broadcast regularly to the French, who listened at their peril on clandestine radios, while Sefton Delmer, the former *Daily Express* foreign correspondent, sowed doubt and despondency on the Continent by organizing 'black' broadcasts to demoralize the German Army. From May 1944 'PsyOps', a branch of the Political Warfare Executive, produced a propaganda paper entitled *Nachrichten für die truppe* ('News for the Troops') which went through 345 editions: 2 million copies were dropped every day over Europe.

By May over a hundred *Messages personnels* were being broadcast to resistance cells every day after the evening news bulletins at 1915 and 2115 hours to trigger a specific response to a pair of phrases implying 'get ready', and then 'act': *'Jean a de longues moustaches'*, *'L'heure du combat viendra.'*

Opposite: Churchill tank removing Belgian Gates.

BELGIAN GATES

Gates – 10-ft high and on rollers – had been towed onto the beaches to form a barrier some 250 yards from high tide, the outermost and largest of the metal obstacles. Tarred Teller mines were lashed to the upright supports. However, at dead low tide between 400 and 700 yards of open tidal flats would be exposed, and this gap in German thinking could be exploited.

Inland the gates were used to block beach exits, lanes and roads. In the open expanses of Utah there were very few gates. They were known as 'Belgian' because, it was said, the metal used had come from redundant defences swept aside in 1940 (as in 'Czech hedgehog' – see page 72).

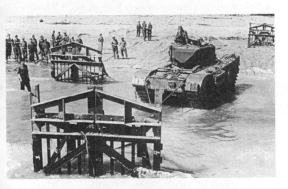

BIGOT

BIGOT was the highest level of security, reserved for those documents and personnel who were privy to the secret of when and where D-Day was to strike. The name came from the high security material sent to Gibraltar (TOGIB) on its way to the North African campaign. Those with BIGOT clearances worked on Allied staffs scattered around London and southern England: one secret location was inside Selfridges, the department store. A bemused response to the question, 'Are you bigoted?' meant that person was clearly not privy to the secret of Overlord. So restricted was the BIGOT project that when King George VI visited a command ship and asked what was beyond a curtained compartment, he was politely turned away. As a sentinel officer later put it, 'Nobody told me he was a Bigot!'

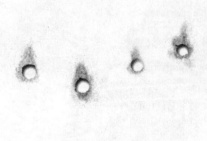

BOLERO

The arrival of 'the Yanks' in the UK began on 26 January 1942. By June 1944 1.5 million men and 2.5 million tons of equipment were in place. The *Queen Mary* and the *Queen Elizabeth*, steaming at 30 knots, could bring a division at a time (16,000 men), the *Aquitania* 8,000 men at 22 knots. The ships initially had to cross the Atlantic unescorted, relying on speed and ULTRA (see page 128). By 1944 a quarter of all weapons and vehicles used by the British Army were American.

This American abundance had an enormous impact in the UK. Some black GIs, with wicked humour, convinced their very white hosts they were night-fighting troops given a special chemical to darken their skin! Some Brits muttered the Yanks were 'over-paid, over-sexed and over 'ere', to which Americans would reply that the Brits were 'under-paid, under-sexed – and under Ike!'

'Yank' gush: 'I come from Bragg!,' proffering a Lucky Strike.
'Limey' muttered reply into his warm beer: 'Yes, I can believe that.'

Of 4,453,061 Americans sent to ETO (European Theater of Operations), only 0.024 per cent were lost at sea.

BOMBARDONS

The Department of Miscellaneous Weapons and Devices, nicknamed 'Wheezers and Dodgers', was headed by Lieutenant Commander Robert Lochner RN. The Bombardon was his experimental sea-calming boom, first 'conceived' in his bath. Twenty-four 200-ft long steel cruciform rafts had seawater trapped in the three lower fins. The ends were anchored at 10 fathoms and linked by rope and chain to form a mile-long breakwater a mile seaward of the Phoenix. The choice of name (which translates as 'let's pelt, bomb or shell' in French, used, for example, in demonstrations against work) proved unfortunate, for when the worst storm in 40 years struck, on 19 June, the rafts tore loose and acted like gigantic battering rams, inflicting fatal damage on the American Mulberry at Vierville, Omaha. The 20,000 tons of precious steel used in their construction was only good for scrap.

BOMBE

These huge electro-mechanical cryptanalytical machines
were first developed by Polish codebreakers in 1938.
They provided the first solution of any wartime ENIGMA
setting, on 17 January 1940. The British model, developed
in August 1940, had 12 times the power of the Polish
Bombes. Continually upgraded, by 1944 there were 200
Bombes of five types, each 2-metres wide and 2-metres
high, operating in several country house locations.
Each was fitted with rows of revolving drums to process
the coded messages. They have been reconstructed at
Bletchley Park in Buckinghamshire, the home of British
code breaking during the Second World War. Hut 11A was
known by the Wren operators as 'The Hell Hole' as the
machines generated a great deal of heat and in the summer
there was no choice but to strip down to one's underwear –
British 'staying power' indeed.

A week before departure, the War Office distributed *Instructions for British Servicemen in France* to everyone taking part in the invasion. The booklet depicted a malnourished and beleaguered people. It gave advice on how to speak and behave, partly to avoid embarrassment but mainly to foster good relations:
'If you should happen to imagine that the first pretty French girl who smiles at you intends to dance the can-can and take you to bed, you will risk stirring up a lot of trouble for yourself – and for our relations with France.'

Some comments remain very true, even today:
'There is a widespread belief among people in Britain that the French are a particularly gay, frivolous people with no morals and few convictions ....'

'The French are more polite than most of us. Remember to call them Monsieur, Madame, or Mademoiselle – not just "Oi!"'

Montgomery had ordered the British to leave their gas masks and anti-gas kits behind, but the Americans continued with every precaution: CC-2 chloroamide compound was applied to their smelly and uncomfortable battle fatigues. The first two regiments of the assault divisions and engineers carried Neoprene gas masks in a waterproof black rubber bag, a tube of British Anti-Lewisite eye ointment, an anti-dim cloth to keep eyepieces clear, two plastic eyeshields, and two gas-detecting shoulder brassards, 5 million having been obtained from the British in reverse lend-lease. Anti-gas hoods and gloves were ready but carried in with general supplies later. Standing by were 60 days' supply of gas shells. It all proved to be unnecessary: Churchill had never believed the Germans would use gas, as the threat of massive retaliation over German cities was very real and very ready. Both sides held massive stocks of what are now termed 'weapons of mass destruction', but for delivery the Allies held the advantage: one fifth of Harris's bomber fleet was adapted in anticipation.

BRUTUS

Roman Garby-Czerniawski was one of the greatest individual contributors to the success of Overlord. He was a Polish officer who had escaped to France in 1939 and set up an espionage network there until, as a result of treachery, he was arrested in November 1941. In July 1942 he allowed himself to be recruited as a spy for the *Abwehr*, who faked his 'escape', but as soon as he arrived in England he worked for the XX Committee (see page 140). (The *Abwehr*, the German military intelligence agency, taken over by Himmler and the *Sicherheitdienst* in March 1944, was an institution in disarray, clogged by credulity.) On 18 May Garby-Czerniawski joined the HQ of FUSAG (see page 60), acting as Polish liaison officer with access to Poles in formations preparing for departure. By D-Day the entire FUSAG chain of command had been revealed to the Germans, but it was all fake.

This extract from Lord Byron's narrative poem *Don Juan*, written in 1819, has often been noted for its striking evocation of a sea-change in history at H-Hour (0630+), when a full moon was required for light and for its effect upon the tides. The 'Post-House' was an inn where the horses were changed at speed to maintain the momentum of long journeys. We are left today with the 'post-obits of theology ...'.

> 'Twas on a summer's day – the sixth of June –
> I like to be particular in dates,
> Not only of the age, and year, but moon;
> They are a sort of post-house, where the Fates
> Change horses, making history change its tune,
> Then spur away o'er empires and o'er states,
> Leaving at last not much besides chronology,
> Excepting the post-obits of theology.

> 'Twas on the sixth of June, about the hour
> Of half-past six – perhaps still nearer seven ...
> a summer's day –
> Summer's indeed a very dangerous season,
> And so is spring about the end of May;
> The sun, no doubt, is the prevailing reason ...

CARBORUNDUM

This abrasive grease was supplied by SOE to a 16-year-old *résistante* called Tetty. She, her boyfriend and her 14-year-old sister sought out the swan-necked flatcars concealed in unguarded railway sidings around Montauban, where the *Das Reich* panzer division was stationed. They siphoned off the valuable axle oil, replacing it with the paste. This was also a great way to earn some pocket money on the black market as the oil commanded high prices. On D-Day the *Das Reich* was ordered to move, but none of the flatcars was serviceable – and the nearest were 100 miles away. With FFI (see page 52) actions triggered by the BBC, it took the Germans 17 days to reach the Normandy front.

After being ambushed and attacked by resistance groups, in a fit of pique they obliterated the quiet village of Oradour-sur-Glane and its 642 inhabitants, and hanged 99 'partisans' from the lamp posts of Tulle en route. Oradour remains as it was left on 10 June 1944, a burnt-out ruin.

The word 'casualty' is frequently confused with fatality. A man is 'lost to battle' because of death, wounding, trauma, shock, psychological dysfunction, illness, accident. He may have gone missing or been taken prisoner. He may turn up later safe and sound. Battle deaths made up a third of casualties. Penicillin, mass produced for the first time, saved many lives. Surgery had made great advances since the First World War and tented army hospitals were prepared, 124,000 hospital beds being imported from the US in kit form and set up on a huge scale; the first hospitals were in place in Normandy on 10 June. Most casualties were the result of grenades, shells, mortar bombs and shrapnel bursts rather than small arms fire, provoking wounds which were often fatal if to the head and abdomen.

How many casualties were there on D-Day?
One half a per cent of those involved, around 4,300 British and Canadians, and 5,700 Americans, a third of the anticipated number. Sources differ: most refer to 630 on Sword, 961 Canadian and 243 British for Juno, 413 for Gold, 2,000–3,000 for Omaha, and 197 for Utah. Low totals start at 8,443, highs reach 10,865. Of these about 2,500–3,000 Allies were fatalities. Airborne casualties, who were much more likely to die from wounds or capture, have been estimated at 2,500 American and 1,500 British and Canadian. The total loss of aircraft and gliders in-

flight involved in the flanking airborne assaults was about five per cent. Casualties among the navies and air forces were extremely low.

German casualty estimates vary widely, reported at anywhere between 4,000 and 9,000.

Civilian casualties across Normandy were of the same order as Allied military casualties (781 being burnt in Lisieux, for example) but greater in the country as a whole.

Source: *D-Day Encyclopedia* (Helicon)
Cross-Channel Attack, G. Harrison (William S. Konecky Associates)

CHOCOLATE SQUARES

The chequered appearance of the concrete squares that made up the access ramps used to facilitate landing craft boarding earned them the nickname 'chocolate bars' or 'chocolate squares'. Large amounts of these 'chocolate bars' gave the soldiers the 'hards', a characteristic port slope for ease of access.

A typical LCT loading schedule called for troops to reach their assigned hard-standing site around midday Saturday 3 June. Loading, checking lashings and casting off took about 30 minutes. After topping up with fuel and water, the craft would cast off from the hard and proceed downstream to an assigned anchorage. Sunday morning brought horizontal rain and the craft returned to port for shelter. Stuck in their open landing craft, some men were seasick two days before they ever got to the Far Shore.

COLONEL WARDEN

This was the code name for Winston Churchill during his many trips around the world. On the day he was forced to leave France, 13 June 1940, he had promised to return to a free France. On 5 June 1944 Winston and his wife Clementine dined together and afterwards he went over to the Map Room in the Downing Street annexe. When she

Above: Churchill and Montgomery, Juno Beach, 12 June 1944.

joined him he said, 'Do you realise, Clemmie, that by the time you wake up in the morning 20,000 men may have been killed?'

His remark may reflect his anxieties born of Gallipoli in 1915, a futile beachhead leaving over 250,000 casualties on both sides. On 3 June 1944 he went to visit the soldiers disembarking at Southampton. An eyewitness described the scene:

'The old man was in his element. He moved among the vehicles talking to everybody. The troops laughed at his sallies and some of them were not slow in answering him back. Many of them touched his coat as they passed and called for a speech. He did not want to speak, he was too full of emotion, so he called out, "Good luck boys."

A soldier called out, "Have you got a ticket, sir?"

"What ticket?" asked Winston.

"One like this," said the soldier, holding up a piece of paper. "It entitles me to a free trip to France."

Much moved, Churchill replied, "I wish I had, if only I were a few years younger, nothing could have kept me away." The tears came to his eyes.'

COLOSSUS

The Colossus was the world's first electronic programmable computer to read ENIGMA and FISH. Three were operational by D-Day, ten by 1945. Each machine was 16ft long, 12ft deep, 8ft high, a 'Heath Robinson' arrangement of cogs, pulleys, punched tape winging through pulleys at over 30 m.p.h., reading 5,000 characters per second (although 'with parallel processing the bit-processing rate could be five times this'. Mark I (Feb 1944) had 1,500 valves, Mark II (May 1944) 2,400, which far exceeded the number in any previous electronic device.

Intercepts spelt out German understanding of the Allied invasion threat at the highest level, and their strategies to counter it. Deceiving the Germans was one thing, but *knowing what they were believing* was the trump card. The machines in the Normandy theatre of war alone were dealing with an average of 4,840 signals per day, requiring 1,000 of the 7,700 staff at Station X to translate and prioritize them as ULTRA.

Source: 'C', Anthony Cave Brown (Macmillan)

In Operation COLUMBA wicker boxes, each containing a homing pigeon, were parachuted into France. A farmer would find a box along with instructions on caring for the bird and fixing a message to the pigeon's leg using the tiny canisters supplied, plus a list of questions the Allies wanted answered: What was being built? What was German morale like? What units were stationed where? The Germans understood their purpose and took to shooting them down – or launching falcons – with at times disastrous consequences for the message sender (as well as the pigeon).

The military also used homing pigeons. 'Gustav' was awarded the Dickin Medal in 1944 for a 5 hour 16 minute flight of 150 miles from Normandy to Thorney Island. He bore the news that the landings had been successful, and later inspired the film *Valiant*. The medal is on display in the D-Day Museum, Portsmouth.

CONDOMS

The Pliofilm clear plastic sleeves known as 'elephant condoms' were robust but made the rifle impractical to carry as they covered the sling as well as the weapon. The answer lay in the standard condom: placed over the muzzle, it could be shot through with no problem. Condoms were used to waterproof cigarettes and matches, letters, currency, even wallets. The rubbers were much larger than the modern version, and fulfilled the task – at a stretch – but did not last long before they tore.

It always paid to keep a few spare for what Montgomery referred to as 'horizontal refreshment'. Once ashore this could be obtained for the price of a few cigarettes, a Hershey bar or some siphoned-off petrol. Montgomery, aware of the high casualty risk from VD, ordered brothels to be closed, but it simply went on in the fields so the activity may not have been as consistently horizontal or refreshing as he supposed.

A 30-ft diameter, 1,600-ton, floating bobbin called a Conun Drum (re-baptized by the Navy HMS *Conundrum*) unwound HAMEL pipeline as it crossed the Channel between Lepe on the mainland and Cowes, then 70 miles from Shanklin to the Fort de Querqueville, Cherbourg. The drum was towed by two powerful tugs. The procedure only took ten hours, but it would be more than 100 days before there was any result. Two lengths were eventually laid to Cherbourg.

In 1945 the PLUTO project came into its own. Eleven HAIS and six HAMEL lines were in place into the Pas de Calais, making a total of 780 miles. By July 172 million gallons of fuel had been pumped across the sea, and the foundations laid for many future peacetime applications. In Normandy seeping petrol supplied a free 'leak in the countryside', and a vibrant *marché noir* (black market) trading fuel for Calvados.

See: www.combinedops.com

COPPERHEAD

Lieutenant M.E. Clifton James, a failed actor, was dressed up and sent to Gibraltar and Alger to parade as Montgomery. But no one was fooled. 'I was as much like a victorious general as a hypnotized rabbit!' he later averred. An alcoholic and heavy smoker, he managed to slip a bottle of gin into his coat, and got stoned with sleeping pills. The flight lasted two hours and he had to be stripped, slapped, made to vomit, swung into the slipstream, doused in cold water and walked up and down to provide some semblance of the teetotal Montgomery upon arrival. But after the official reception he was seen drunk and smoking cigars, lodged in his prosthetic right hand (the result of a First World War wound). After the war he returned to his Pay Corps clerical job, unable to explain or justify his five week absence. He later re-emerged in the 1958 film *I was Monty's Double* alongside John Mills.

The initials stand for Combined Operations Pilotage Parties. X20, a four-man midget submarine commanded by Lieutenant K.R. Hudspeth DSC, brought in Major Logan Scott-Bowden DSO, MC and Sergeant Bruce Ogden-Smith DCM, MM. Between 17 and 21 January 1944 the coast was observed by day by periscope, and soundings taken; at low tide the boat settled on the seabed to conserve power.

Each man was weighed down with a shingle bag, brandy flask, sounding lead and stake as he swam ashore equipped with small arms and knives, a .45 revolver, rubberized canvas wetsuit, torches, ballpoint pens (invented for use under water), writing tablets, watches and compasses, all waterproofed with periscope grease or held in condoms.

Their mission was to check for peat, clay and shingle deposits that could hinder vehicles on shore, spot exits and sea walls, measure gradients with fishing lines and stakes, and take samples with 18-inch augers, all under the noses of the German guards. Benzedrine tablets kept them going. Later in the month Bowden warned General Bradley that the future Omaha Beach was 'going to be a very tough proposition indeed'.

One hundred of 470 surviving U-boats still threatened the NEPTUNE fleet. The Dover Straits would therefore be sealed off by minefields, and the Western Approaches to the English Channel protected by a massive air patrol system, code named Operation CORK, flown by the 19 squadrons of long-range aircraft in No. 19 Group, based in Plymouth. In order for U-boats to emerge from bombproof silos in the Atlantic French ports they needed to be able to 'breathe' at the surface every 30 minutes. Consequently, from 18 April Coastal Command flew missions every half hour, day and night, between Ireland (hence CORK) and the Bay of Biscay. No U-boat was able to operate in the English Channel in June and by 25 July they had sunk only nine Allied ships – but Coastal Command had lost 60 aircraft.

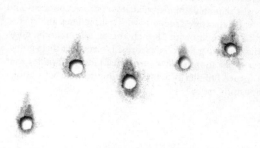

COSSAC

Chief Of Staff, Supreme Allied Command. Lieutenant General Sir Frederick Morgan was appointed at the Casablanca conference to draw up the draft plans for an invasion known as Operation ROUNDUP, an assault into Normandy of three divisions, and two parachute brigades over Caen. Montgomery preferred a much larger attack of six divisions and three airborne divisions over 60 miles of coast with a coherent strategy of breakout. This was Overlord, ready in outline by 1 February 1944. That there were tensions created by his 'broom' are hinted at in his memoirs, which state that men like Morgan 'considered Eisenhower as a god … he placed me at the other end of the celestial ladder'.

Under Eisenhower, COSSAC became SHAEF, the Supreme Headquarters of the Allied Expeditionary Force.

CROSSWORDS

Beginning on 2 May 1944 a series of clues in *The Daily Telegraph* crossword announced to the world the most secret code words of the war. Had security been compromised? Each code word appears in this book:

2 May *Daily Telegraph* crossword 5775, 17 across:
  One of the US
22 May crossword 5792, 3 down:
  Red Indian on the Missouri
27 May crossword 5797, 11 across:
  But some bigwig like this has stolen some of it at times
30 May crossword 5799, 11 across:
  This bush is the centre of nursery revolutions
1 June crossword 5801, 15 down:
  Britannia and he hold to the same thing

The author of the crossword, Leonard Dawe, a prep school teacher in Surrey, was detained and questioned by MI5. He said he had compiled the crosswords some months earlier. It was put down to an incredible coincidence. Dawe died in 1963. In 1984 a former schoolboy, Ronald French, broke ranks (and an oath of secrecy imposed by Dawe) and said he had helped provide words and that schoolboys had easy access to the 'sealed' camps thereabouts, where code words were picked up without realizing their true signficance.

Answers on page 101

According to Eisenhower, the C-47 (or DC-3 civilian airliner) was the most important aircraft of the Second World War: he nicknamed it 'the Willing Slave'. It carried out 1,400 missions on D-Day, and 400 resupply flights on D-Day+1. Unarmed and unarmoured, rugged and reliable, it could carry 18 paratroops or an 8,000lb load. It could fly at 230 m.p.h., but would slow to an unnerving 80–100 m.p.h. to allow men to jump from a side door at 450 feet. It took 10–15 seconds to reach the ground. The risks were revealed to the author in 2004 when, in an historic re-enactment outside Sainte Mère Église, a parachute failed to open, an accident known as a Roman Candle.

Forty-two C-47s were destroyed on the first two days of operations but most crews survived and were returned to Allied control. The low casualty rate among the crews of IX Troop Carrier Command was a source of tension with some of the US paratroops.

The terms D-Day and H-Hour go back to 1918, when they were first used at the battle of Saint-Mihiel by the American Expeditionary Force to describe the day and hour the attack was opened. Leaving blank an undated reference to the Day (D-) and the Hour (H-) contributed to security: the Germans would be aware of the preparations of the opening of the Second Front, but the exact intended time would have been known only to very few Allied planners. In any case, 'the Day' was displaced from 1943 to 1944, and then twice that year: from 1 May owing to a shortage of craft and material, and from 5 June due to the weather, so the practicality of this shorthand is self-evident.

The system also allowed events prior and following the pivotal moment to be referred to as 'minus' and 'plus'. Hence one week before D-Day would be D-7; two hours after the initial assault would be H+120.

Used extensively in the Second World War, the sense has, since 6 June 1944, been dominated by that of the opening Day of Operation Overlord.

Day of Days, Decision Day, Disembarkation, Deception, Deliverance: the blank is there to be filled by the imagination – thanks to D-Day.

44

When Station X heard that the 17 divisions of the German Fifteenth Army were on their way from the Pas de Calais area, GARBO was instructed by 'C' (Sir Stewart Menzies, head of M16) to send a warning to Berlin; it reached Hitler on 9 June: 'Should the Fuhrer be tempted to move his army out of Calais it would be a mistake; as soon as he did so FUSAG would make its move.' On 10 June, at 0730 hours, Hitler rescinded the order to move the Fifteenth Army and ordered reinforcements into the Pas de Calais area.

When his orders were read out as an ULTRA decrypt, Field Marshal Alan Brooke (Chief of the Imperial General Staff, or CIGS) said, 'If Hitler is such a bloody fool why is it taking us so long to beat him?' He then stalked out of the room.

Erwin Rommel (1891–1944). Inspector in Chief of the European continent's defences in November 1943, and from January Army Group B Commander of Seventh Army (seven divisions) and Fifteenth Army (17 divisions). His boss was Field Marshal von Rundstedt. Both were insistent that no extra forces should be released to Normandy from the Pas de Calais. After showing great drive and optimism in strengthening the defences, Rommel gave himself a break. On 4 June, with the prospect of poor weather for two whole weeks, and the armies stood down, he left his HQ at La Roche Guyon, north-west of Paris, for his home in Herrlingen, near Ulm, 800km away. The next day he learnt that he would be allowed to see Hitler on the 8th regarding the deployment of tanks closer to the beaches. His wife Lucie's 50th birthday was on 6 June so he had bought her a pair of shoes in Paris. At 0730 hours the phone rang ... it was Speidel.

DIVISIONAL NICKNAMES

Some divisions that landed on D-Day and D-Day+1:

ALL AMERICAN:
82nd Airborne Division (Utah), Major-General Matthew Ridgeway

BIG RED ONE:
1st Infantry Division (Omaha), General Clarence Huebner

BLUES AND GRAYS (and, after two years training in the UK, ENGLAND'S OWN):
29th Infantry Division (Omaha), General Charles Gerhardt.
The colours refer to the old North and South, reconciled.

INDIAN HEAD:
2nd Infantry Division (behind 1st ID), Major-General Walter Robertson

IRONSIDES:
3rd Infantry Division (Sword), Major-General Tom Rennie (Monty's old Division)

IVY LEAF:
4th Infantry Division (Utah), Major-General Raymond Barton

RED DEVILS:
6th Airborne Division (Sword), Major-General Richard Gale

SCREAMING EAGLES:
101st Airborne Division (Utah), Major-General Maxwell Taylor

TOUGH OMBRES
90th Infantry Division (behind 4th ID), Brigadier-General Jay MacKelvie

TYNE AND TEES/'FIFTY DIV':
50th Northumbrian Division (Gold), Major-General Douglas Graham

The only 'Funny' (see page 59) used by US forces, the amphibious 32-ton Duplex Drive Sherman tank was intended to spearhead the beach assault ahead of the troops, pick off bunkers and provide cover for engineers.

A collapsible rubberized canvas folding screen attached to the waterproofed hull was raised 13ft on struts by means of compressed air. While still at sea, the tank was driven out of an LCT (Landing Craft Tank) and two 16-ft propellers were engaged to proceed at 4 knots; fully laden, the freeboard was just 8 inches. A periscope allowed the driver to peer over the screen and operate a tiller-rudder. Ashore, transmission could be shifted to the treads and the screen deflated to fire at targets while still seaward of the beach obstacles. Some tanks thereby flooded *in situ* as the tide rose. The psychological impact on the defenders of a tank rising out of the sea must have been considerable, but results on D-Day were mixed. If disembarked close in, as at Gold and Utah, all was well, but if not the choppy seas spelt disaster.

DUCKS

Born out of the need to load banana ships in remote places (the head of OSRD, the US Office of Scientific Research and Development, having worked for the United Fruit Company before the war), the amphibious 'duck' shuttled small stores from ships to transfer areas ashore. Loaded, it had a 12-inch freeboard.

DUKW is not an acronym, but a GMC (General Motors Corporation) code: D = 1942 U = Utility K = all-wheel drive W = two powered rear axles. In fact 90 per cent of its parts were common with a standard GMC two-and-a-half ton truck. The huge tyres could be inflated or deflated according to need, an innovation in 1944. They served on D-Day as artillery platforms and appeared ashore quite early on – but not in the first waves, as appears in *The Longest Day* (see page 87).

One of the 200 Ducks in Arromanches harbour went missing but returned several days later. Its crew of two had pushed off to see their girlfriends in England, but were not punished as their major had always enjoined them to use their initiative!

ENIGMA

The ENIGMA machine, which looks like an elaborate old typewriter, had been adopted by all the German armed forces by 1935. The Poles had already reconstituted the ENIGMA in 1932 using two manuals supplied by the French Secret Service, who had in turn obtained them from Hans-Thilo Schmidt, a German Army cipher operative. When the ENIGMA machine raised the bar by going from three to five rotors in 1939, the Poles passed a five-rotor machine to Station X to be examined. Through a series of 26 letter contacts between the cogged rotor wheels and an electrical plugboard, some 140 trillion combinations were eventually possible, confirming the Germans in the belief the machine was impregnable. It was essential they continued to believe so.

Right: ENIGMA –
decrypts showed what the
Germans knew.

FFI

Free French Forces of the Interior, a term used by De Gaulle after the landings to denote all the disparate *résistance* forces prepared to work against a common enemy. There were about 3,000 *résistants* in Normandy, but cells were active all over France. The networks were often divided, betrayed and infiltrated by the Gestapo, particularly in Normandy. By themselves they could make little difference, but funded, guided and trained by SOE, and by meeting the Allies' military needs, these fragile cells of resistance could and did make a valuable contribution. In May 1944 alone 3,700 secret reports were sent to England about German installations and, on receipt of coded messages from the BBC, on the night of 5/6 June eight bridges and over 100 vehicles were destroyed, as well as many railway and telephone lines. *Résistants* could also assist air crews behind the lines and guide Allies to military objectives.

FIRST GENERALS

FIRST ALLIED GENERAL TO DIE

Brigadier General Don F. Pratt, deputy commander of 101st Airborne Division, was in the first wave of 104 Waco gliders. He was sitting in a raised position on his parachute in a jeep, itself strapped with nylon ropes to the plywood floor, when the glider slithered on the dewy grass and crashed into poplar trees near Hiesville at about 0345 hours. His head hit an overhead strut and his neck was broken. One of the pilots was also killed. Pratt is buried in Arlington. The crash was reconstructed in the film *Saving Private Ryan*.

FIRST BRITISH GENERAL IN FRANCE

Major-General Richard Gale, commander of 6th Airborne Division, landed a Horsa glider, *Chalk* No. 70, in a large field of stubble at about 0330, along with 67 other gliders and four Hamilcars. On his way to Ranville he picked up a white horse, so rode into France's first liberated village. He lived to 1984.

FIRST GERMAN GENERAL TO DIE

Generalleutnant Wilhelm Falley, commander of the 91st Anti-Airlanding Division, drove back at speed with two staff officers from his interrupted war game in Rennes. He approached his HQ, the Château de Bernaville (Manche), just as Lieutenant Malcolm Brennen, commander of the

508th PIR (Parachute Infantry Regiment), was asking the owner directions, having just landed nearby with four of his men. They opened fire as the staff car appeared and the vehicle crashed into the house. Wounded and spread out on the road, Falley reached for his pistol. After a shouted warning, Brennen shot him dead. A huge Nazi flag found in the car is displayed – folded – in the Airborne Museum, Saint Mère Eglise. Falley is buried in Orglandes Cemetery (Manche).

FIRST GENERAL ASHORE
Brigadier General Theodore Roosevelt Jnr, the eldest son of US President Theodore Roosevelt, declared that 'his men would feel safer if there was a General with them'. Aged 56, and in poor health, he landed at H-Hour on Utah Beach, only to suffer a fatal heart attack on 12 July – just as he was due to assume command of the troubled 90th ID. Roosevelt has become the Normandy American Cemetery's most famous interment, one of three individuals there awarded the Medal of Honor, and is buried [D:28:45] next to his brother Quentin [D:28:46] who was killed aged 21 in an air action on 14 July 1918.

FIRST ARMY, GENERAL
General Omar Bradley was the soft-spoken General whose reserved style earned him the sobriquet the 'GI's general'. He had a painful boil on his nose and asked not to be photographed or filmed on D-Day. He lived until 1981.

FIRST FAKE UNITED STATES ARMY GENERAL (FUSAG)

General George S. Patton flew into Le Ruquet airfield (Omaha) in secret on 6 July when his very public role as head of FUSAG was passed briefly to General McNair. Patton assumed command of the Third Army on 2 August, to carry the momentum begun on Operation COBRA out of Normandy and into the rest of France. Patton's neck was broken in a car accident in December 1945, and after a lingering and painful death he was buried in the US Luxembourg Cemetery [P:1:1].

FIRST US GENERAL TO BE KILLED BY OWN SIDE

Lieutenant General Lesley McNair briefly took over Patton's role running FUSAG as the German belief persisted. Responsible for training America's citizen army worldwide, he observed the launching of Operation COBRA, the breakout on 25 July, and under 5,000 tons of American bombs was killed along with 111 men. He lies in the Normandy American Cemetery [F:28:42], the most senior US officer killed in action during the Second World War to be buried overseas. In 1954 he was posthumously promoted to full General. His son, Colonel Douglas McNair, was killed by a Japanese sniper on 7 August 1944 and is buried in the Honolulu Military Cemetery.

FISH

FISH was the name given to decrypts of the *Geheimschreiber*, the 'Secret Writer' developed to protect the highest level of communications with a 12-rotor system. The Lorenz SZ40 produced TUNNY, the Siemens T52 *Geheimschreiber* STURGEON – both types of fish. Von Rundstedt's codes were called JELLYFISH. These were communications of the highest order, between Armies, Army Groups and the German High Commands, and included messages to and from Hitler himself.

A phone call from Hitler to Baron Oshima, the Japanese Ambassador in Berlin, on 30 May showed he believed in FUSAG and thought a 'feint' might be attempted outside the Pas de Calais. Unfortunately, Station X's link with Berlin became unreadable shortly after D-Day, and in July they also lost JELLYFISH, which had been cracked in March and which had been delivering valuable signal intelligence (SIGINT). FISH decrypts were recovered only in October 1944.

Opposite: Patton's Army was equipped with light tanks.

FORTITUDE

Operation FORTITUDE South: to concentrate German efforts in the Pas de Calais, the Allies equipped FUSAG with inflatable life-size military *materiel*. Shepperton Film Studios constructed fake oil terminals, airfields filled with balsa bombers, landing craft made of canvas, oil drums and scaffolding poles ('Big Bobs'), and even created lighting to simulate troop concentrations. There were royal visits, and communications from a fleet of signal vans broadcasting in codes the Germans were known to be able to decrypt.

There was also a FORTITUDE North, to convince the Germans a fictional Fourth Army would attack Norway first, with strategic Soviet support. According to this fiction, FORTITUDE South would follow in the Pas de Calais in mid-July. After D-Day, Normandy was presented as a feint to draw German reserves away.

'In wartime ... truth is so precious that she should always be attended by a bodyguard of lies.'

(Winston Churchill)

The brainchildren of Major-General Percy Hobart, this was the term used to denote the odd-looking profiles of the armour specially adapted for D-Day. The 'Beware of the Bull' insignia of 79th Armoured Division was well known as these Armoured Vehicle Royal Engineers (AVREs) were embedded in many British and Canadian units.

The Sherman CRAB flail tank thrashed the ground with chains spinning from a projecting drum in order to trigger mines.

The Churchill CROCODILE squirted liquid flame over a range of 80 yards and towed a trailer bearing 1,800-litres of pressurized fuel.

The Churchill GREAT EASTERN was a 4.8-ton bridge operated hydraulically and lowered over streams, ditches, anti-tank walls, etc.

A roll of chestnut paling known as a BOBBIN MAT could be unrolled forward of the Churchill FASCINE tank.

The Churchill PETARD or FLYING DUSTBIN was armed with a 290mm spigot mortar to fire a 40lb charge up to 80 yards and shatter concrete.

The ARK, a Churchill Armoured Ramp Carrier, was designed to bridge defence ditches and sea walls.

FUSAG

The First United States Army Group was established in October 1943 as the follow-up formation that would move to France once the lodgement area had been secured. Many of its divisions were already in south-east England, so the idea was promoted to suggest that they were being made ready to spearhead the cross-Channel attack at its narrowest point.

FUSAG was commanded by General Omar Bradley – but double agents made it clear that General George S. Patton was in charge as it was known that the Germans anticipated Patton would command the main assault. His speeches and movements were scripted. The timing worked perfectly, as Patton was to lead the Third Army and was not due to cross to France until July. By June 1944 it appeared to the Germans that there were twice as many Americans in the UK than was in fact the case. They were still taking the threat seriously in late July – by which time FUSAG had evaporated.

GAMBIT

On 4 June, using a combination of an echo sounder, an 18-ft telescopic mast with a light shining to seaward, and a radio beacon, two four-man midget submarines, X20 and X23, guided in the leading flotillas of the British and Canadian assaults and checked on the position of the flotillas and the DD tanks. Americans declined their use, trusting to the accuracy of their own techniques. The 24-hour delay added to the crews' discomfort and to the considerable risk on a lee shore that their batteries would fade while countering the current ahead of H-Hour, leaving the submarines to wash up on the beach. The crews spent 64 hours dived out of 76 hours at sea. Gambit or gamble?

GARBO

Juan Pujol Garcia (1912–88), Spanish and anti-fascist, convinced the Germans and, later, the British that they should employ him as a secret agent. In 1944 he was awarded the Iron Cross – and the MBE. His first reports, under the code name ARABEL, detailed wartime British life to his German controller, Karl-Erich Külenthal, but in fact came out of Lisbon. Duly impressed, MI5 set him up under the code name GARBO in a suburban house in Hendon, north-west London, where a fictitious network of 27 sub-agents, known as ALARIC, was created. They operated in areas from where credible intelligence could be gathered for passing on to Berlin (who footed the bill for this fiction!). He sent over 500 reports to the Madrid section of the *Abwehr*, and it worked: German estimates of the number of FUSAG divisions present in south-east England were put at 75.

It was good for morale for generals to be known by folksy nicknames:

Beetle was Major-General Walter Bedell Smith (1895–1961), Chief of Staff, SHAEF

Bimbo was Lieutenant General Miles C. Dempsey (1896–1969), Commander British Second Army

Desert Fox was Field Marshal Erwin Rommel (1891–1944), Commander Army Group B

GI's General was Lieutenant General Omar Bradley (1893–1981), Commander US First Army

Harry was General Henry Duncan Crerar (1888–1965), Commander First Canadian Army

Ike was General Dwight D. Eisenhower (1890–1969), Supreme Commander AEF

Lightning Joe was General J. Lawton Collins (1896–1987), Commander VII Corps Utah

Monty was General Bernard Law Montgomery (1887–1976), Commander Twenty-First Army Group

Ol' Blood 'n' Guts was General George S. Patton (1885–1945), Commander Third Army

Speedy was Brigadier Stanley James Ledger Hill (1911–2006), Commander 9th Para

Tubby was Major-General Raymond O. Barton (1889–1963), Commander 4th ID

Windy was Major-General Richard Gale (1896–1982), Commander British 6th Airborne Division.

GOLD

The westernmost British sector was divided into Jig and King beach, each a mile-and-a-half long, and 25,000 troops landed here. The 50th Northumbrian Division, beginning at 0725 hours, was later strengthened by the 7th Armoured Division after D-Day. In King sector lay the Mont Fleury casemated 4 x 150mm gun complex, indicated by a key marker, known as the 'Lavatory Pan', a house with a circular drive set back from the beach.

The area was attacked by the Green Howards, and CSM Stan Hollis took 30 prisoners in clearing an enemy trench, and later outside Crépon earned the only VC of D-Day by drawing fire to himself in order to save his comrades.

Mont Fleury turned out to be a building site, and the garrison fled. There were 413 casualties. In nearby Ver sur Mer the Gold Beach Museum tells the story.

Source: British Army Operational Research Group

GOOSEBERRY

This was the name given to 72 heavily ballasted old merchant ships set out to scuttle themselves in controlled explosions (with the crews on board). The purpose was to form breakwaters bow-to-stern off each of the five Landing Beaches and allow smaller craft, Rhino ferries and Ducks to shuttle to shore in the lee of their beached hulls. Each ship was called a Corncob, and they were all in place by 11 June 1944.

After Mulberry and Gooseberry, one naval wag proposed Raspberry as a code word, but this was discounted as a little ripe; Churchill strongly disapproved of flippant code names for military operations.

THE GREAT PANJANDRUM

The most deranged D-Day invention conceived and tested at the Combined Operations Experimental Establishment (COXE) at Woolacombe, North Devon, was the Great Panjandrum: two 10-ft rocket-powered wheels joined by a hollow drum containing 4,000lbs of explosive. This was ignited inside the landing craft and the ramp lowered so it careered up the beach at 50 m.p.h. like a berserk Catherine wheel and burst through the sea wall. It was a total flop, and was not used in Normandy.

The most practical was perhaps the simple Tankdozer, an adapted Sherman with a bulldozer blade for shovelling obstacles into piles, ready to turn Hedgehogs into Rhinos.

(ALSO KNOWN AS CORPORAL SCHICKELGRUBER)

A derogatory name for Hitler used by German soldiers in 1944: *Größter Feldherr aller Zeiten*, meaning 'the greatest war lord of all time', was originally used in Nazi propaganda after the fall of France in 1940. For the first two hours into 6 June 6th Hitler was still in conference with Goebbels at Berchtesgaden. Back at his own hotel just two hours later Goebbels received news of a possible invasion, but the Führer was not woken until around 0900 hours – which for Hitler was early.

While 1600 Panzers awaited orders to move, Hitler took a bath and then departed for a midday conference at Klessheim castle, an hour's drive away, with General Döme Sztojay, the Hungarian Prime Minister since 23 March. Over an interminable vegetarian lunch Hitler pronounced on his confidence in victory, on his secret weapons, the V1s, which he ordered fired, and expressed pleasure at the progress being made on 'the Jewish question'. Over the previous three weeks, beginning on 15 May, 12,000 Hungarian Jews were being transported to Auschwitz every day. On 15 June Sztojay ordered a further 200,000 into ghettos. By 8 July (when the deportations were stopped by Admiral Horth) 437,402 Jews were

Opposite: Lieutenant Nevil Shute (the novelist and designer) at beach trials.

recorded by the Reich Plenipotentary *SS Brigadefuhrer* Edmund Veesenmayer (1904–77) as removed to Auschwitz in 151 trains – half of the entire Jewish population of Hungary murdered in seven weeks. Non-smoking and mostly vegetarian, Hitler apologized for the inconvenience his health considerations imposed on lunch: 'The elephant is the strongest animal there is and, you see, he doesn't like meat!'

General Warlimont, Chief of German Army Operations, recalled, 'As we stood about in front of the maps and charts we awaited with excitement Hitler's arrival and the decisions he would take. Any great expectations were destined to be bitterly disappointed. As often happened, Hitler decided to put on an act. As he came up to the maps he chuckled in a carefree manner and behaved as if this was the opportunity he had been awaiting so long for to settle accounts with the enemy.'

Hitler suddenly released the Hitlerjugend ('Hitler Youth') and Panzer-Lehr to Rundstedt's command, but no infantry reserves. The orders did not get through until about 1600 hours, and the tanks were not able to move in daylight. Then he returned to the Berghof, to take his usual walk to the Tea House, and was ready for an afternoon nap. The delay would prove fatal for the outcome of the Battle of Normandy and the survival of the Third Reich.

The terms H-Hour and D-Day describe the hour and day the attack opened (see page 44).

H-Hour was set for about an hour after daybreak and dead low water: 0630 for US beaches, 0725 for the British, 0745 for Juno. The preparatory bombardment would lift five minutes beforehand, then DD tanks would go in first. The Engineers, a third of the initial force, needed to clear the beaches dry-shod and mark the cleared lanes with flags. A rising tide eased the task of retracting landing craft, the full tidal range being 18–24 feet. Half way along the 60 mile landing zone, dead low tide was 0525. At Juno the tidal surge of the 5 June storm helped lift the first waves over the Calvados reef offshore, but a further 10 minute delay was still required. At Utah it allowed the LCVPs an extra kilometre run-in over the almost-flat shallows of the bay of the Vire river. However, on Omaha the obstacles were being swamped ahead of schedule. H-Hour saw stiff offshore north-west winds of force 4–5 (15–20 knots), 3–6ft waves, clearing cloud cover, a 2.7 knot tidal current, an abating winter storm.

HAM AND JAM

These were the code words announcing the first mission of D-Day had been successful. Six Horsas and their tugs, bearing 180 men of the Ox and Bucks Light Infantry led by Major John Howard, took off from Tarrant Rushton in Dorset at one minute intervals, starting at 2256 hours, and were cast off 75 minutes later. Howard's lead glider *Chalk No. 91* landed 47 yards short of the bridge.

Within minutes the garrison was overwhelmed and the bridges taken. While awaiting reinforcements from 7th Para, Sergeant 'Wagger' Thornton, 'trembling like a leaf', deployed his single short-range and unreliable PIAT (Projectile Infantry Anti-Tank) bomb and repelled the armoured counter-attack, destroying the lead tank and encouraging the rest to withdraw. Two men were killed and 17 wounded in the initial assault (plus three civilians), but only 76 men were unwounded by the end of the day.

HAMILCAR

This was a 68ft-long 7-ton (18,000-lb) glider that could carry an 8 ton load – armoured vehicles, guns, or a Tetrach tank. Only the Halifax bomber could tow it. It had a hinged nose, designed so that the weight of the cargo tipped the aircraft forward on landing, so no ramp was needed. The two pilots sat in a cockpit on top, protected by bulletproof glass and an armoured floor. The crews of the vehicles or tank inside sat in them during the crossing and started up their engine(s) while still in flight. A special canvas tube to the outer skin carried the exhaust outside. There were no losses.

Of the three types of 850 gliders deployed, the Hamilcar was the safest, it was beautiful to fly and all but four came in on the daylight attack. In all, 25 American and 34 British glider pilots were killed, 65 wounded and 162 seriously injured; 53 became POWs.

HEDGEHOG

A beach obstacle made up of three metal beams welded or riveted together in order to rip a hole in the landing craft, or block its approach and hold it in the killing ground of the beaches. Many had concrete footings to make them harder to push aside. Staggered, overlapping rows of Hedgehogs were sited 130 yards out, each row being about 100 yards long with 15 obstacles.

An hour before high water they would be submerged. It was the job of the Engineers to demolish them and the other beach obstacles before the incoming tide hid them, and mark the cleared lanes with flags. They were also known as 'Czech Hedgehogs' because they recycled steel from the redundant defences of the Czech Sudetenland.

'The damnedest country I've seen' (Bradley), a terrain of enclosed fields, deep ditches and thickly rooted embankments topped by dense hedges. The French term is *bocage*, a *boc* being an enclosure. Tanks could not traverse it and they left men and *matériel* exposed in the country lanes to pre-sighted mortar and artillery fire. The single cattle entrance to each field provided the perfect target and special means had to be developed to overcome a well-entrenched and determined enemy who had had four years to familiarize himself with the terrain. Allied planners underestimated the difficulty of fighting in such close country and the time it would take to overcome it. For the gliderborne assault it presented small landing zones, for tanks no field of fire. But it did provide the airborne with plenty of close cover to hide and harass, and German tanks lost their advantages of range. The difficulty of the country cut both ways once battle was engaged.

Andrew Jackson Higgins designed the famous 'Higgins Boat', but Higgins Industries in New Orleans also produced the dashing PT boat and the first effective LCT. The 'hard-fisted, hard-swearing and hard-drinking' Higgins became a powerful shipyard owner, with seven plants and 20,000 employees, manufacturing 20,094 LCVPs alone. He paid his workers equal rates, regardless of race, sex, age or disability, according to their function. Across the US, 25 other plants produced Higgins Boats royalty free.

In front of a crowd of thousands, on 23 July 1944 Higgins staged a re-enactment of D-Day à l'Américaine (complete with aircraft) in New Orleans to celebrate the delivery of his 10,000th boat. A stray firework set fire to his suit and ruined it. After the war he was ruined as well.

HORSA

This 3-ton glider could carry up to 29 men, or 3 tons of *matériel* (a 6-lb field gun and limber, a jeep and trailer, motorbikes, etc.). Quick-release bolts in the fuselage frame allowed the rear to burst cleanly away and *matériel* to be driven out on rails: getting clear quickly was vital. There were 12 in the first lift that were fitted with a pair of arrester parachutes for the *coup de main* operations (normal landing speed was 90 m.p.h.).

Constructed in perforated plywood and corrugated cardboard, with a detachable tricycle undercarriage, and central skid, they were thought safer than Wacos as they absorbed impact better. But they were nicknamed 'Flying Coffins' by the infantry, who had no idea that many had been assembled by coffin manufacturers!

Horsa gliders were also used in the daylight glider lifts in the US sector, but the open countryside in the British sector made for better landings than the 'hedgerow country'. A huge 97 per cent of all gliders were used once; they were only good for firewood after the landing. There were 325 gliders used in the British assault.

IKE

General Dwight D. Eisenhower (1890–1969), Supreme Commander of the Allied Expeditionary Force, code named LOOK, showed a rare genius for coordinating the activities of inter-Allied staff. Appointed on 6 December 1943, he became a symbol of Anglo-American friendship and cooperation, the 'chairman of the board': 'Teamwork wins wars.' He was responsible for four key decisions: to go for the Transportation Plan; to adopt a broad front to the overall strategy; to deploy American Airborne forces in large numbers; and the final decision to go. He was

made personally responsible for the security of ULTRA. Suffering from tinnitus, four packets of Camel cigarettes a day kept him going, but he worried about the inexperience of so many troops, and about 'grey, fat World War One colonels and officers'.

In an iconic picture of Operation Overlord he is seen going to Greenham Common in Berkshire to see off the US Airborne. During the informal walkabout he spoke to a blacked-up Lieutenant Wallace C. Strobel:
'Where you from?'
'Saginaw, Michigan.'
'I've been there and liked it. Good fishing there!'
Morale was high, but back in the Cadillac he remarked to his driver Kay Sommersby, 'It's very hard really to look a soldier in the eye when you fear that you are sending him to his death.'

JEDBURGHS

Jedburgh teams consisted of an Englishman, an American and a Frenchman or Belgian trained in guerilla tactics, leadership and in demolition work, especially railway infrastructure, and all 2,000 wore uniform. Their purpose was to provide support for local resistance wherever they landed and try to coordinate local efforts in the best interests of Allied strategy.

They got off to a disastrous start, however. QUININE and AMMONIA (a wag named them after patent 'medicines') were the first teams to be launched on 5 June, but their pilots were unable to pinpoint the Drop Zones and had to return to base. The Ops were remounted on 9 and 10 June. There were 13 teams dropped into France in June 1944 (six of them in Brittany) and 70 followed over the next ten weeks. None was captured and none betrayed, but 21 men were killed, nearly all in gun battles with the enemy.

JUBILEE

This code name comes from the Hebrew, and means 'rejoicing trumpeted from rams' horns'.

In the Dieppe Raid of 19 August 1942, 4,963 Canadians, 1,075 British and 50 US Rangers, 252 ships and craft, five destroyers and 74 RAF squadrons attacked the Upper Normandy port to test its defences. Many never even reached the shingle beach and the tank treads jammed on the pebbles. Reinforcements were sent in to further slaughter: 907 died, half at sea; 586 were wounded and 1,946 captured. In the town of Winona, Ontario every serviceman was a casualty. The British lost 45 men, with 466 becoming POWs. The RAF lost 106 aircraft (five by friendly fire) in the largest dogfight of the war to date. The Navy lost 33 naval vessels and one destroyer. The Americans were bloodied for the first time in Europe: 13 casualties. In total there were 4,259 casualties. Von Rundstedt wrote to Hitler, 'They will never try that a second time!'

What were the lessons learnt for Overlord?
The following were identified: the need for improved air and naval firepower and radio coordination; the need to bomb the coast first; the need for specialized landing craft and armour, for harbour facilities of their own, for radar jamming and diversionary landings, for sandy beaches

and not pebble ones and, above all, for absolute secrecy. Getting all these factors right led to the remarkably low casualties of D-Day. Lord Mountbatten claimed that the success of Overlord was won on the beaches of Dieppe, but it has been said this is like justifying the *Titanic* disaster on the grounds that it led to improved ship design.

Difficulties with the Calvados offshore reef meant 'Force J' was delayed by 10 minutes and landed at 0755 hours. To the east lay Gold Beach, and the British and Canadians were separated by LOVE. The 3rd Canadian Infantry Division landed either side of Courseulles, at MIKE and NAN. Their phase lines inland were called YEW, ELM and OAK (the Caen–Bayeux road). The 21,400 men, which included 6,000 British troops, took over 1,200 casualties on D-Day on the second most heavily defended beach. 'Bloody Buron' lay just ahead, Kurt Meyer's three battalions of 12th SS panzer division and panzer Mk IVs. Over the next two weeks the 3rd Division played a crucial role in brutal confrontations around Caen, drawing enemy reinforcements onto their front. Canadians who had volunteered for overseas service at the outbreak of war did not see their country for over five years.

KRAMER V. CRAMER

General Hans Cramer (whose name is sometimes seen spelt as 'Kramer') of the Afrika Korps, Knight of the Iron Cross, was a POW in England in 1944. He was returned to Germany on the grounds of ill health as it was an opportunity to get the message across that Operation FORTITUDE wanted the Germans to believe: that the landings were focused on the north of France, not Normandy.

Driven through the vast D-Day preparation areas, Cramer was made to believe he was in south-east England. All the road signs had long since gone. The 'indiscreet' conversations between the 'driver' and his 'companion' were scripted. Cramer was interviewed at Kensington Palace then dined with Patton, the most 'indiscreet' of them all. Returned via Sweden through the Red Cross, he was taken immediately to Berchtesgarden and appointed Hitler's Special Adviser to OKW West, the HQ of all German armies in western Europe. After all, who could be more trustworthy?

Opposite: Landing craft moored in Southampton docks.

LANDING CRAFT

By far the biggest single problem that faced the Western Alliance with respect to D-Day was manufacturing and allocating a sufficient number and variety of landing craft. The key to success was the variety of adaptations to specific tasks. (If over 200ft long the craft or boat became a ship, in naval parlance.)

APA: Attack Transport
LBE: Landing Barge Emergency Repair
LCA: Landing Craft Assault (British)
LCE: Landing Craft Emergency Repair
LCF: Landing Craft Flak
LCG: Landing Craft Gun
LCH: Landing Craft Headquarters
LCI: Landing Craft Infantry
LCK: Landing Craft Kitchen
LCM: Landing Craft Mechanized
LCP: Landing Craft Personnel
LCR: Landing Craft Rocket: 792 rockets in 24 salvoes
LCT: Landing Craft Tank: six tanks maximum
LCVP: Landing Craft Vehicle and Personnel
LSD: Landing Ship Dock
LSE: Landing Ship Emergency Repair
LSH: Landing Ship Headquarters: floating command posts for each beach
LSI: Landing Ship Infantry
LST: Landing Ship Tank
XAP: Assault Transport Craft

LARGE SLOW TARGET

A loaded Landing Ship Tank lay in barely one metre of water at the bow and three metres at the stern, making it almost impossible to sink. A lift connected the upper deck to the lower. At 100 metres long, it could carry 20 tanks or 120 small vehicles, plus around 200 troops. It could be beached at 10 knots, or unloaded at sea onto Rhino ferries, which was quicker and safer. The LST was an ocean-going ship known to its crews as the 'Floating Brick' because of the uncomfortable ride. The sole remaining D-Day LST 325 is moored in Evansville, Indiana.

A total of 233 were used on D-Day, 59 British and 174 American. No LST was lost before 8 June, when one was mined; two were torpedoed from E-boats next day. Two others were later sunk by mines.

LCVP

The Landing Craft Vehicle and Personnel would carry a 30-man assault team or a 3-ton vehicle, had a crew of three and a range of about 100 miles. A total of 1,089 LCVPs were used on 6 June. They were usually carried on a larger transport ship and reserved for the first waves. Larger craft and landing ships would arrive once the immediate danger was overcome. From about 0250 hours the LCVPs began to be lowered into the water for the final run-in; it was too dangerous and tiring to cross the Channel in these craft.

With the flat-bottomed LCVP bucketing in the 5–6ft waves for four hours, filled with standing men and all their equipment, seasickness and cramps aboard were common. A swift disembarkation was difficult, and at times men fell out on grounding.

THE LONGEST DAY

The words are attributed to Rommel during an inspection:
'The first 24 hours of the invasion will be critical ... the
future of Germany will depend on the outcome ... for the
Allies as well as for Germany it will be the longest day.'
Cornelius Ryan's 1959 book and Darryl F. Zanuck's 1962
film of the same name are classics, but in the film we see
American paratroops jumping from Lancaster bombers,
Rangers climbing the cliff at midday and fighting on
its crest around the monument to their own heroism in
the evening, German pilots jumping into two unarmed
post-war sports planes (the Bf108 Taifun), and French
commandos filmed on the harbour front in Port en Bessin
(Gold) attacking the Ouistreham casino (Sword) – which
had been demolished before D-Day.

See www.imdb.com/title/tt0056197/goofs

MICKEY MOUSE MONEY

'Occupation money' was issued to every soldier in the invasion just before departure, in order that he might have currency negotiable with the French once ashore: each received 40 five franc notes, along with a helpful booklet on France. Some of the more cynical soldiers thought it yet another elaborate deception, but the notes had been printed in 1938.

On the eve of D-Day General de Gaulle made the currency issue a matter of national sovereignty and declared it and AMGOT (Allied Military Governance Overseas Territories) null and void as far as France was concerned. Currency for him was a central symbol of independence. *'Allez, faites la guerre avec votre fausse monnaie!'* ('Just go ahead and fight your war with your fake money!'), he retorted to Churchill in their 4 June meeting.

The currency was indeed met with suspicion by the French and circulated little: they paid their taxes with it, while the soldiers nicknamed it 'Mickey Mouse Money'.

Opposite: Monty's first press conference in Normandy, 11 June 1944.

General Bernard Montgomery (1887–1976). Monty's immense battlefield experience and training made him the obvious choice to command the land forces of 21st Army Group. Despite his frosty relations with Americans and others, the success of D-Day must be attributed to him. With the clout and drive he possessed, he increased substantially the forces deployed. A hard taskmaster, who promoted realistic, even life-threatening, training, his self-confidence and showmanship made him hugely popular with his troops and the British population. Always confident and gifted, and possessing the charisma to communicate with soldiers and factory workers alike, he came to symbolize the Allied commitment to victory in Europe. However, Montgomery's habit of regarding superiors as an interference made Eisenhower's job harder, and he called Monty 'a good man to serve under, a difficult man to serve with, and an impossible man to serve over'.

Montgomery's favourite biblical quotation was 'For if the trumpet give forth an uncertain sound, who shall prepare himself to the battle?' (1 Corinthians 14:8)

MOONSHINE

Positioned at night in the Dover Straits, 18 launches produced augmented radar images that suggested a large surface fleet. As they advanced under low-level dumps of Window (see page 138), they towed huge floats known as 'Filberts' to which were tethered 30-ft long barrage balloons in the style of LSTs. Some 10 miles from the enemy coast, huge loudspeakers were used to broadcast the pre-recorded sound of anchor chains rattling through the hawsers of capital ships, and smoke was generated. At daybreak the Germans, in a state of high alert and alarm, looked out across the Boulogne Straits at an open, empty sea.

MULBERRY

Churchill's plan to tow flat-bottomed concrete barges to the Frisian Islands dated from 1917. Two 'prefabricated' harbours, one for each army, would allow the Allies to dispense with a frontal attack on an existing port and land in the open bay of the Seine, then assure supplies in all weathers and tidal conditions. Each day 5,000 tons were planned to go through Mulberry A (American), 7,000 tons through Mulberry B (British), plus 2,500 vehicles. There were 300 companies building them, a million tons of concrete being poured and 45,000 men being put to work. Everything would be towed after D-Day from the 'Near' to the 'Far' Shore and the essentials be in place by D-Day+14. Mulberry A was destroyed in the Great Storm of 19–21 June, but eventually 42 per cent of British supplies came through the British harbour, which was quickly baptized Port Winston: he visited it in the greatest secrecy on 12 June, and 20–23 July, staying on board HMS *Enterprise*, keen to see the elaborate workings of what he termed 'my synthetic harbour'. Mulberry was so secret its very existence was not admitted until the end of October.

The fine museum in Arromanches was the first in Normandy on the D-Day theme and opened in 1954.

See www.combinedops.com
www.musee-arromanches.fr

'MY MASTER PLAN'

Montgomery liked his plans to be simple in conception and execution. His orders were verbal, and he detested paperwork and 'frigging about'. Win the air battle first, launch the attack at the place of your choosing, and maintain the initiative. Kill Germans. 'In its subsequent operations the Army will pivot on its left (Caen) and offer a strong front against enemy movement towards the lodgement area from the east.' The taking of towns for their own sake was immaterial; what mattered was to allow the US Army to break out 'southwards towards the Loire', 'directed on to Paris' (his notes of 7 April). The failure to take Caen for over a month caused deep and lasting resentment. The hinge straddled Caen, instead of turning south of it, but it was not in his character to admit that everything did not go according to the letter of his Master Plan: 'I am bound to make enemies whatever I do. I shall go on doing my duty, come what may.'

NEPTUNE

Orders were written out on 900 close-typed pages and summaries printed into 22 volumes. Rear Admirals Vian and Kirk led the Eastern and Western Task Forces under Admiral Bertram Ramsay (of Dunkirk fame). Convoys began assembling in radio silence from 18 May. In all, 1,213 ships and 736 ancillary craft, with 4,126 landing craft, shuttled 132,000 troops to the Far Shore with hardly any loss or interference. There were 78,244 British and 20,380 US naval personnel in the warships, 32,880 US and 30,009 Royal Navy personnel in smaller craft, with 4,988 from other Allied countries. Around 25,000 crewed the 864 merchant ships; 79 per cent of the fleet was British. The German Navy was absent except for three torpedo boats from Le Havre, one of which sank the Norwegian destroyer *Svenner* on D-Day (34 men were lost). The Luftwaffe stayed away: the barrage balloon over each of the larger craft was unnecessary.

HMS *Belfast*, the 10,000-ton cruiser now moored near Tower Bridge in London and open to visitors, was one of 106 bombardment ships and is one of the last major ships to survive from NEPTUNE. It provided fire support for Juno Beach from 0527 hours, engaging batteries at Ver sur Mer and Courseulles. By 14 June it had fired 1,996 six-inch rounds, and continued to provide fire support in the Caen area until 11 July.

See www.iwm.org.uk/visits/hms-belfast

What was the attitude of the local population?
In Normandy the Germans were a good source of barter
and trade, and it paid to cooperate: they paid for what
they took, respected the women, and were regarded, at
least in the early years of occupation, as *'correcte'*. Vicious
reprisals followed any acts of resistance. Passive resistance
was not uncommon but also carried risks. After four years
of occupation, *attentisme* prevailed – wait and see.

After the landings the Allies, subject to strict rationing for
years, were struck by the quantities of butter, milk, cream,
meat and eggs. But for six months Normandy was isolated
and the dairy products had nowhere to go. The *patisseries*
sold cream but no cakes, since flour was unavailable.

The mass of civilians were undeniably friendly to their
liberators, but jubilation could be followed by ugly scenes
of retribution against collaborators and women who had
consorted with the Germans. Around 150,000 babies in
France had German fathers.

A return to routine saw the re-establishment of a right to
complain: the Allies paid less well, mistreated local women,
were laggard in clearing the fields of mines; there were
shortages of everything, outside markets being cut off for
months; and so on. The Norman peasant remained close

to his wallet. But civilian needs were great, Normandy being left ravaged by the three month battle. Half a million buildings were destroyed, 14,000 civilians killed, and many more were wounded and traumatized. It is said that the women were more likely to accept the harsh cost of liberation than the men, and be forgiving: '*On ne fait pas d'omelette m'sieur, sans casser les oeufs.*' ('You can't make an omelette without breaking eggs, monsieur.')

Source: André Heintz, *grand résistant* in Caen
Occupation, Ian Ousby (Pimlico)

OMAHA

Omaha had unique characteristics: a 4-mile long sandy bay flanked by cliffs and backed by 100–170ft-high bluffs; five wooded valleys, or 'draws', led inland. On the return of each draw were *Wiederstandsnest* (strongpoints) providing cross-, plunging and enfilade (end-to-end) fire. They were manned by a recently arrived division, the 352nd. The Blues and Grays' 116th Infantry Regiment's objective, draws D1 and D3 (DOG), was barred by a paved promenade beach road and its supporting sea wall; the Big Red One 16th Infantry Regiment's, E1, E3 and F1 (EASY and FOX), faced a Dieppe-style 8ft-high coarse shingle bank and anti-tank ditches. The Engineers were to clear sixteen 50-yard wide lanes through the beach obstacles and de-mine the bluffs.

These geographic characteristics assisted the vast enterprise of beach-landed logistical support once the battle was over.

What went wrong at Omaha Beach?
The brief naval bombardment began around 0540 hours; visibility was made poor by smoke and dust and the 13 enfilading defensive positions were well protected and reinforced by the 352nd Division. The 14-inch guns of the USS *Texas* were wasted on the Pointe du Hoc; 480 B-24

Opposite: High tide on D-Day: an Omaha follow-up wave.

bombers dropped 1,285 tons of bombs through cloud 3 miles inland; 27 DD tanks sank before reaching land; an offshore current and rising tide covered the untouched mined obstacles and shunted men away from their planned objectives. The absence of 'Funnies' (see page 59) was felt keenly. Around 10,000 LCR rockets largely landed short, radios failed, and demolition parties were unable to work. It looked as if the assault might unravel as a brief paralysis set in. At 0830 hours General Bradley, on board USS *Augusta*, requested his men be landed elsewhere, and the Germans reported victory in the sector. Despite these huge disadvantages, the infantry carried the day and established a slender beachhead, but such was the disruption that it took six days before the V Corps had casualty figures logged: by 12 June, 1,225 were killed of 5,846 casualties, with 457 of the dead being buried by the beach road on DOG WHITE.

OVERLORD

This code word was deliberately chosen for its air of ringing authority: it covered the plans, preparations and the campaign to open the Second Front in Europe. Its most striking symbol was the Overlord stripes painted on all the aircraft. The air fleet consisted of 5,049 fighters, 3,467 'heavies', 1,645 medium and light bombers, 2,316 transports, 2,591 gliders and 698 other aircraft. On the last weekend, after the camps were sealed, paint and brushes were handed out to apply black and white stripes to the fuselage and wings in order to reduce friendly fire incidents in the air or from Allied anti-aircraft positions on the ground. It announced the imminence of D-Day – just as the mission was postponed from the planned Monday. Over 50 tons of black and white paint were used on the aircraft, and so much had to be done so quickly that planes were left with characteristic ragged edges to their stripes.

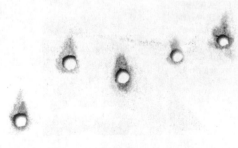

PBI

British Army slang for 'Poor Bloody Infantry'. By May 1944 the British Army had reached the limits of its growth, two and three-quarter million men, while the American Army numbered five and three-quarter million, with an inexhaustible supply to call upon. By 1943 Britain was recruiting men in their 40s, 30 per cent of the working male population was in the armed forces, and there were 450,000 women in non-combatant roles associated with D-Day. For the Battle of Normandy, Montgomery was told he would have reserves to draw upon for a month. This alone justified his well-known reluctance to squander lives. The existing divisions would have to be 'cannibalized' if casualties were heavy, and replacements found from existing resources.

Awaiting them on the Continent were the formidable, experienced and courageous fighting men of the German Army: better led, better at killing, and outclassing the Allies on the ground in every respect save artillery and transport.

British and Canadian troops numbering 75,215 were landed by sea on D-Day.

PEGASUS

This nickname is attributed to Daphne du Maurier, wife of the founding general of the British airborne forces, Lieutenant General Frederick 'Boy' Browning. Its military code, EUSTON I, denoted a heavily guarded 1933 cantilever bridge over the Orne canal linking Caen to the sea. The seizure of this bridge intact, and the Horsa river bridge nearby, EUSTON II, was considered so vital it was the first

Above : Pegasus bridge on 7 June 1944.

mission of D-Day in uniform. Success would make it possible to send forces landed at Sword beach across the Orne canal and river to reinforce the British airborne forces. The dividend of keeping the D-Day secret would be first paid out here. An excellent museum perpetuates the memory of the British airborne operations and preserves the original bridge.

See www.memorial-pegasus.org

Crossword answers

2 May *Daily Telegraph* crossword 5775, 17 across:
One of the US: answer Utah

22 May crossword 5792, 3 down:
Red Indian on the Missouri: answer Omaha

27 May crossword 5797, 11 across:
But some bigwig like this has stolen some of it at times: answer Overlord

30 May crossword 5799, 11 across:
This bush is the centre of nursery revolutions: answer Mulberry

1 June crossword 5801, 15 down:
Britannia and he hold to the same thing: answer Neptune.

PHOENIX

These were 212 hollow concrete boxes in six sizes, 204ft long and weighing from 1,600 to 6,044 tons, constructed on 28 sites in south-east England. They took four months each to make, using 600,000 tons of concrete and 31,000 tons of steel. They were gathered into two assembly areas off Dungeness and Selsey Bill, 'parked', pumped out, and on a given signal were towed, four a day at 4 knots, each by a single tug, to the Far Shore. From 8 June they began to arrive and, once nudged into position, they were 'planted', sea cocks being opened to allow water to flood in. In 22 minutes the unit settled to form part of an offshore breakwater for a Mulberry. When choosing the code name for the harbour, no one had noticed that the role of the Phoenix was spelt out to the world in Luke 17:6: 'And the Lord said, If ye had faith as a grain of mustard seed, ye might say unto this Mulberry, Be thou plucked up by the root, and be thou planted in the sea, it should obey you.' (A sycamine in the Authorized Version is the black mulberry tree.)

The remains of the Phoenix have formed the backdrop of British commemorative ceremonies at Arromanches since 6 June 1945, in partnership with the French *Comité du Débarquement*.

PICCADILLY CIRCUS

'Piccadilly Circus' was the area south east of the Isle of Wight where the ships of Operation NEPTUNE were to circle and peel off according to their orders: it was also known as Area 'Z'. South of here, the largest minesweeping operation of the war cleared the 'Spout', a channel 20 miles wide, from Lat. 50°N, for ten lanes of shipping on the night of 5/6 June. Beyond a moored mine barrier 7 to 11 miles from the French coast the sea was clear, so this provided the position for the bombardment fleet, and for the transports lowering their craft. Heavily laden men (68lbs of kit was not uncommon) began to climb down nets and fill the LCVPs and LCAs which, once loaded, circled in their turn, awaiting orders for the final run-in.

Three wartime Disney characters fuel the petrol story:
PLUTO was the Pipe Line Under The Ocean to Cherbourg,
BAMBI the pumping station set up in the rubble of a
Shanklin hotel that served as camouflage, and DUMBO the
Boulogne pipeline link. The name BAMBI was inspired by
some antlers and a stag's head found in the hotel. HAIS
and HAMEL pipelines led off across the English Channel,
HAIS lines being multi-layered flexible lead pipes clad in
57 galvanized twisted steel wires, while HAMEL lines
were 3-inch steel tubes, similar to land-based oil lines.
For security, pipelines were always referred to as 'cables'.
Planned to be in place on D+18, by D+100 there was only
1,500 gallons of fuel ashore at Cherbourg!

Four ex-merchant ships laid the HAIS pipeline but
persistently failing mechanical couplings on the ships,
poor weather, untrained crews and the many booby traps
and mines in Cherbourg harbour meant the first pipeline
was not successfully connected at both shore ends until
18 September. This was also the date the first Liberty
ship docked alongside a restored Cherbourg quayside.
The petrol flowed on 22 September but was turned off on
4 October as attention became focussed on DUngeness
and BOulogne, hence DUMBO. PLUTO was operational
for just 13 days and made no contribution to the Battle
of Normandy, although 'PLUTO Minor' operated into

Port en Bessin (Gold), pumping oil ashore from offshore tankers. By July 1945 PLUTO had contributed 10 per cent of imported fuel to Europe.

Isigny sur Mer, heavily damaged by naval bombardment, lies between Omaha and Utah sectors, and, curiously, is the ancestral home of the Disney (d'Isigny) family.

See www.combinedops.com

PRAISE THE LORD

This was the code name communicated by reflector lantern at 0730 hours from Colonel Rudder's cliff-top HQ 320 yards east of the Pointe du Hoc; around 180 Rangers (of 250) had made it to the top. Within the hour the mission would be accomplished. All this, despite losing the British-crewed LCA 860 and 21 men at sea (recuperated safely), their supply craft LCA 914 with all their rations and ammunition (with five men on board) – and their way: pilot Lieutenant Colin Beever RNVR in ML (Motor Launch) 304 lacked the usual navigational training and equipment and took them towards the wrong 'Pointe' (de la Percée, 3 miles east). They landed 38 minutes late, but thereby missed an accurate, delayed B-26 bombing run at 0645. About 15 men were cut down crossing the shoreline reef. The landing at 0708 caused the 650 men of 5th Ranger Battalion to land at DOG WHITE on Omaha Beach, where they were ordered to reinforce Vierville (DOG GREEN) until 8 June.

The book and film *The Longest Day* (see page 87) 'cheated the Rangers of recognition for their contributions to the success of the Normandy invasion'.The American Battle Monuments Commission, together with over a million visitors each year, and recent scholarship, has put this right.

Source: *Rudder: From Leader to Legend,* Tom Hatfield, Texas A&M University Press

Photographic Reconnaissance provided 80 per cent of the information on the German fixed defences. Oblique photography was possible from high shutter speed cameras under disarmed and turbo-charged reconnaissance USAAF P38 Lightnings, and RAF Mosquitos and Spitfires operating at very low levels, augmented with visual observations by RAF Mustangs. This revealed that in Normandy, from February 1944, the Germans were not only laying minefields on land and on the beaches, but also demolishing ports and quaysides, casemating coastal batteries with reinforced concrete, preparing to flood low-lying areas, and setting up scattered lines of Hedgehogs, tripods, gates and other devices a short distance below the high tide line.

Between 1 April and 5 June 5,000 Overlord reconnaissance sorties were flown, and over 10,000 prints were processed through the night of 6/7 June alone.

PUNCH AND JUDY

Punch and Judy were the drop codes that allowed men to recognize each other in the dark as they formed up for the mission to take the Merville battery, thought to contain four 155mm guns threatening Sword Beach. Two hours after the drop only 150 of 750 paratroops were ready to attack. None of the three gliders was able to land within the perimeter as planned and the heavy bombing had missed the casemates. Led by Lieutenant Colonel Terence Otway, without jeeps, trailers, mortars, engineer support or mine-clearing equipment, they charged the battery anyway and lost half their men in capturing it but found old Czech 105mm guns. The guns had been spiked before withdrawing. Commander of 9th Battalion, Brigadier James 'Speedy' Hill's own party of 42 men, misdropped in the flooded Dives valley, was bombed by the RAF while trying to get back to the safety of their own lines, and everyone was killed or wounded.

'Gentlemen, in spite of your excellent training and orders, do not be daunted if chaos reigns. It undoubtedly will.'

(Brigadier Hill)

An acronym for RAdio Detection And Ranging.

A total of 92 German radar stations were set up in northern France. Of 47 radar stations in operation three weeks before D-Day, no more than six were able to transmit on the vital night and they picked up Window (see page 138) confirming the disembarkation of FUSAG towards the Pas de Calais. By now, only one station was working in the invasion area itself, at Douvres la Délivrande, Calvados, and its report was discounted as no other stations were confirming it! This is now a radar museum.

Y-Stations picked up the trace of 23 German radar jamming centres but this proved to be an error: PR confirmed only five and these were destroyed on the night of 2/3 June. The German Air Force's Signal Intelligence headquarters for north-west France was also knocked out.

RAF Lancaster and USAAF Flying Fortress bombers blocked the real airdrops by dropping a wall of Window and blasting out communications jamming.

The Allied fleet had 800 ships and craft equipped with effective radar-jamming equipment, including some landing craft that were purpose-built jamming platforms.

'*Wir haben starke RADAR-störungen!*' (We are having major radar problems!) The English acronym used for radar jamming in the film *The Longest Day* would have been unknown at the time. Germans spoke of *Funkmeßgeräte* (radio measuring equipment).

On D-Day the Germans in the air were not only absent, but blind.

Source: *Most Secret War*, R.V. Jones (Penguin)

Marshal Philippe Pétain (1856–1951), the First World War hero, was head of the 'French State' operating from the spa town of Vichy from 10 July 1940. Jews were actively hunted down, and compulsory labour service in Germany served upon 2 million Frenchmen. Another 2 million were already POWs. De Gaulle was condemned to death *in absentia*.

Pétain visited Paris on 26 April 1944 and was acclaimed by hundreds of thousands. He sat in attendance on a Requiem Mass, held in Notre Dame Cathedral and presided over by Cardinal Suhard, in memory of the 3,000 civilians killed in Allied air raids over the previous two weeks. Within four months General de Gaulle was standing at the same spot – being shot at while everyone else fell to the ground.

After the war Pétain was tried and condemned to death; however, his sentence was commuted to life imprisonment and he lived out his days in prison on the Ile d'Yeu, dying at the age of 95.

Source: *Petain's Crime*, Paul Webster (Pan Books)
N.B. It proved too late to correct 'a real salad' – the mis-translation of '*un vrai salaud*' before going to print. This was the term used by Robert Badinter, Président du Conseil Constitutionnel, Ministre de Justice; the translation should have read 'a real swine'.

REBECCA/EUREKA

An emitter/receiver guidance system deployed 30 minutes ahead of the main airborne force by Pathfinders. The EUREKA, which was equipped with a self-destruct charge should it fall into enemy hands, sent a signal to the REBECCA receiver to guide the paratroops to the right Drop Zone. Holophane marker lights were also to be set up. It worked well in the British sector, but in the US sector the planes came in scattered. Factors included cloud, ground fire, the need to maintain radio silence, and the over-reaction of the young pilots of the Dakotas, three-quarters of whom had no combat experience and one fifth no night-time flying. Many Pathfinders were misdropped, their beacons broken or lost on landing, or there were simply too many Germans about. And although every C-47 had a REBECCA, to keep from jamming the system with hundreds of signals only flight leads were authorized to use them in the vicinity of the Drop Zones.

The mission for the 7,900 men of the British 6th Airborne Division was to capture intact the bridges over the canal and river at Bénouville, and secure a bridgehead of sufficient depth to hold them. To isolate the area, the four fixed bridges over the flooded Dives river valley were to be destroyed, along with the battery at Merville. 'Holding attacks' on the left (eastern) flank of the assault were to delay further incoming German reinforcements.

The Pathfinders landed from 0018 hours, the main body of paratroops, each bearing about 60lbs of equipment, from 0050, a 500ft drop lasting around 20 seconds. Operation TONGA deployed 373 Dakotas and Albemarles (adapted bombers), of which 359 made it, delivering 4,310 of the 4,512 paratroops. Nine planes were lost and 14 aborted. Of the 98 Horsas in the first wave of gliders, 18 were lost before arrival: ditching over the Channel at night was certain death.

There were 611 infantry on board the first wave when they set out, of whom 493 went into action from around 0320. Three Horsa gliders were planning to land at 0430 on Merville battery, but missed.

Operation MALLARD, landing from 2100, saw 226 Horsas and 30 Hamilcars of 6th Air Landing Brigade despatched; ten Horsas were lost. The sight of this armada caused the Germans to withdraw from their initial counter-attack on the coast between Sword and Juno, believing MALLARD was headed for Caen itself. As many as 98 per cent of gliders landed within 2 miles of target; one in 70 men were killed.

By 17 August, 579 paratroops, 220 gliderborne infantry and 257 men from support units were killed, 102 were missing and 2,743 were wounded.

RHINO

Rhino was a term used to describe two distinct items of military *matériel*: a type of tank and a type of raft.

The first was based on an idea by US Sergeant Curtis G. Culin who proposed adapting the Sherman tank with a 'horn' made from a rack of chopped up Hedgehogs which could bury itself in the thickly rooted embankments of the Bocage, and burst through in a place of its own choosing. This enabled surprise attacks to be launched *en masse*, the enemy not expecting to be attacked by Rhinos fitted with Hedgehogs. The tank no longer exposed its soft underbelly when rising over the embankment. It was not widely used until mid-July.

The other Rhino was a 200-ft by 70-ft, 400-ton raft or pontoon made up of steel 'blisters', that would approach upwind the open bow doors of an LST or LCT, whose ramp would be lowered onto the deck. An LST could be emptied in two shifts. Propelled by two 60hp outboard motors, it could then ferry the heavy equipment – up to 40 vehicles – and beach itself in 3 feet of water. It could also be reconfigured into a floating pierhead to receive docking landing craft, either at sea, or beached alongside.

RONSON

'Buy a Ronson – lights up first time' went the jingle for the famous cigarette lighter. The ease with which an M4 Sherman tank burst into flames when struck by a shell earned it this bleak nickname. The Germans called it (in German) 'the Tommy cooker'. Their shells could go right through it, in one side and out the other. A rather desperate gesture was to weld one-inch armour patches over the three ammunition boxes, under the turret and in front of the driver's periscope. Fast, mobile, reliable, and easy to make and ship, the Sherman was nevertheless no match for the German tank head-to-head. Two thirds of British tanks were Shermans (about 900 on D-Day); many of the rest were Churchills.

What does this film tell us about D-Day?
For 30 minutes we see 850 Irish soldiers attack Curracloe Beach, County Wexford, on 26 July 1997, where the beach obstacles are characteristically pointing the wrong way. We see the 155mm guns of the battery at Longues (Gold) overlooking Omaha Beach, where there were none, Tiger tanks, which first appeared at Villers Bocage (Gold) on 12 June, where there were none, and London bricks in the reconstructed town of Neuville (Hatfield airport), where a ruined Bailey bridge is seen even before the town is 'captured'. However, the representation of death, dying and wounds and the effect of battle on mind and flesh makes a deep impression. *Saving Private Ryan* is to be 'enjoyed' for what it is and appreciated for the attention it has drawn to the sacrifice, heroism and cruelties that were played out in Normandy.

Opposite: A knocked-out Sherman Crab on Gold Beach.

SNAFU

First recorded in 1941, this is an informal and unofficial American Army term whose publishable version is Situation Normal: All Fouled Up.

It reflects the resigned acceptance of men facing a grim situation not of their making, where the incompetence, bad judgement or bad planning is not unexpected. It may also be mocking the Allies' fondness for acronyms and code words in this period.

The Navy had a version that went, 'Situation Normal: Army Fouled Up', to which the Army reply was 'Some Navy Asshole Fouled Up'.

One of the BBC 'Stand By' messages for the resistance on 1 June was '*Les sanglots lourds [longs] des violons de l'automne*' (the heavy [long] sobs of autumn violins). This strophe from the Verlaine poem *Chanson d'Automne,* here corrected in parentheses, told the railway-cutting team Ventriloquist to make ready.

On 5 June, at 2115 hours, among the 110 other Action messages of which about 50 were poem idioforms, the strophe continued with '*bercent [blessent] mon coeur d'une langueur monotone*' (rock [wound] my heart with a monotonous languor).

The Germans correctly assumed this was probably part of a general call to railway resistance and implied an invasion within 48 hours. The Fifteenth Army Intelligence in Lille informed von Rundstedt and La Roche-Guyon, Rommel's HQ. At 2233 hours Fifteenth Army was itself put on standby. But Seventh Army remained unmoved.

SOE

Special Operations Executive, later led by General Sir Colin McVean Gubbins, was set up by Churchill in July 1940 'to set Europe aflame', to carry out clandestine missions of great daring on the occupied European continent in order to irritate the Germans and give comfort to its enemies. It supplied, financed and implicated resistance forces in occupied countries to achieve its aims. In 1943, 1,075 agents and 6,545 tons of weapons and explosives were dropped into occupied territories.

SOE code names for agents operating in France were usually trees (Tilleul, or lime tree) or occupations (Acrobat, Ventriloquist); Gaullist networks used fish (Pilchard); military delegates used French geometrical terms (Ellipse, *Circonférence*); air liaison used the names of weapons; inter-Allied missions used herbs and scents.

'Without SOE the Resistance could have achieved nothing.'
(Max Hastings)

Source: *SOE in France*, M.R.D. Foot (HMSO)

In the evening of 5 June, Rommel had gone home and his Chief of Staff General Hans Speidel was holding an informal drinks party with members of the 'Black Orchestra'. At 1045 hours Speidel received a report from 15th Army Intelligence that the Verlaine strophe had been completed. His guests left at midnight and at 0100 hours he went to bed. Ten minutes later the 716th Division based in Caen was informed and at 0135 hours Speidel was woken by General Major Max Pemsel, the first of a series of calls designed to get Speidel and von Rundstedt to react to the reports of dispersed airborne landings that were coming in. Speidel believed they were nothing more than a local raid; reports of dummy parachutists and captured air crews muddied the picture.

At 0215 Pemsel announced that the sound of engines could be heard off Cherbourg, but von Rundstedt still did not consider it a major operation. He felt there had been too many such warnings before, and the deteriorating weather hardly suggested an imminent landing – reconnaissance flights had been cancelled over the weekend because of it, nor was it expected to improve.

At 0309 hours surviving German radar reported strong contacts at sea in the Boulogne/Baie de Somme area. At 0445 Speidel was advised of the start of aerial bombardment on a massive scale along the entire coast. Key SS panzer divisions made ready but needed Hitler's authority to move. The Allied enterprise had achieved total tactical surprise. Between the American H-Hour at 0630 and the British H-Hour at 0725 Rommel was finally informed by Speidel of what was happening.

After the war Speidel played an active part in NATO; he died in 1984.

STATION X

The code name for GC&CS, the Government Code and Cypher School at Bletchley Park, a Victorian mansion at the heart of an extensive complex of huts outside London where the ENIGMA codebreakers worked and transmitted intelligence. Some 7,723 men and women were serving at Bletchley by 1944, dealing with over 84,000 decrypts a month: Churchill called them the 'geese that laid the golden eggs and never cackled'. It was the Germans' misuse of the ENIGMA machine that made it possible to decipher intercepts, some operators taking short cuts when setting up, which compromised the security of the coded message.

Today Bletchley Park is open to visitors as the centre of computer and intelligence history.

See www.bletchleypark.org.uk

SWORD

West of the Orne canal, seaside resorts such as Ouistreham, Hermanville, Lion and Luc sur Mer cling to the coast. The plan was to land on either side of the villages and head inland to take Caen. German strongpoints overlooking the beaches took the names of fish: Cod, Sole, Pike and Trout. On the Périers ridge, others were given the homely names of British motor cars: Daimler, Hillman, Morris, and Rover – perhaps they thought they would be quickly broken down! Six commando units were deployed to overcome these obstacles, but the goal of 3rd Division (Major-General Rennie commanding) proved over-ambitious. Congestion and confusion on the narrow beach front, stiff German opposition from the sequence of strongpoints, and the need to support the 6th Airborne Division east of the Orne led to delay. A total of 28,845 men landed, taking 630 casualties on the beaches. A month after D-Day Caen, 5 miles beyond the ridge, was still in German hands.

Source: British Army Operational Research Group

The dress-rehearsal for D-Day, code-named Operation Fabius, was in six parts. The first part (Fabius I) was Exercise TIGER, held off the Devon coast at Slapton Sands on the night of 27/28 April. In a dead calm sea a flotilla of eight LSTs bearing engineers and chemical and quartermaster troops, along with their fuel-full trucks, DUKWs, jeeps and heavy engineering equipment, were heading inshore when nine German torpedo 'E' boats, detecting the heavy radio traffic, approached, emptied their torpedoes and withdrew. Three of the LSTs were hit: one managed to limp back to port; a second burst into flames; the third keeled over and sank within six minutes. Trapped below decks, hundreds were burnt; men drowned, weighed down by waterlogged overcoats, or were pitched forward into the water by their own lifebelts. Others succumbed to hypothermia as no rescue came until 0500 hours. The final death toll has been estimated at 946 men.

Ten of the officers were 'BIGOTed' (see page 20). Had any been plucked out of the sea by the E boats? There was no rest until all had been accounted for – grim work for the divers involved. All ten bodies were located, so the secret was safe.

TITANIC

'The buggers have fallen for it' (coded SAS message to base).

The name of an airborne attack with dolls; 29 Sterling and Halifax bombers released 537 Ruperts, a one-third size clutch of sandbags designed to resemble a paratrooper (not resin lookalike dolls as depicted in *The Longest Day*), along with two three-man SAS parties between Omaha and Utah. Verey flares, Lewes bombs, pintail bombs and firecrackers accompanied the drop, while gramophones emitted the sound of small-arms fire interspersed with soldiers' voices. German night-fighters were dispatched to attack the fake airdrop, but couldn't even find it after the communications jamming ('Airborne Cigar') cut off the connection to their ground controllers: none of the transports involved in the true airdrop was attacked.

This small operation had a disproportionate effect: the German 915th Grenadier Infantry Regiment, the reserve of the division holding Omaha Beach, was sent at 0300 hours to investigate the attack. When they returned, the Americans could no longer be dislodged from their narrow beachhead.

All six SAS men were captured on 10 July trying to get through German lines, but survived the war.

TWO CORPS, TWO CORPSES

By 7 June, General Major Max Pemsel, Chief of Staff of the 7th Army, declared that 'the entire scheme of American manoeuvre and order of battle' for D-Day had come into his hands. Two American officers' bodies had been recovered, one in a boat in the Vire estuary, the other near Vierville. Each body carried a briefcase with waterproofed operational orders, one for Utah VII Corps sector, the other for Omaha V Corps sector. This was entirely against Allied security regulations. Pemsel concluded that the Normandy invasion was the main thrust and told his commander, von Rundstedt, and Hitler. The 17 divisions of the powerful 15th Army were ordered to move from the Pas de Calais, and the orders were intercepted by Station X.

ULTRA

ENIGMA decrypts were referred to as ULTRA, since they were ultra secret. The quality of ULTRA varied: it was not always possible to make tactical decisions based upon it, and in the battle it required land lines to be taken down, forcing the Germans to use their radios. The actions of the resistance in the days following D-Day, together with air attacks, accelerated this process, but the mass of ULTRA intelligence came from the Russian and Italian fronts rather than from Normandy.

In 1974 Group Captain F.W. Winterbotham (1894–1990), responsible for getting ULTRA to the commanders in the field, wrote *The Ultra Secret* (source of the entirely specious story that Churchill sacrificed Coventry in 1940 in order to keep the secret safe). Churchill's personal copies of ULTRA, which had been referred to only as his 'secret source' in his writings, were only finally declassified in 1994.

In just 15 hours, 23,250 men, 1,700 vehicles and 1,700 tons of stores were got ashore. Losses of 4th Infantry Division totalled 197, 12 of those killed and 106 of those wounded being soldiers, an astonishing result. The obstacles were not mined, and 4,400 250lb bombs dropped by 275 B-26 Marauders in low-level runs *along* the beach proved accurate. The mislanding 2,200 yards from target saved lives. Of the 32 DD tanks, 28 landed without difficulty, but 15 minutes late and behind the infantry. With the seabed at TARE–UNCLE almost flat, the demolition teams had unlimited time to work on clearing the obstacles. Six engineers were killed when a shell struck their craft, but the job was done in an hour despite German artillery shelling from inland. On the high seas an LCT transporting the 29th Field Artillery Battalion hit a mine: 39 men died and 20 of them are listed on the Normandy American Cemetery Wall of the Missing. In 2011 the museum at Utah Beach was rebuilt and enlarged to include a B-26 Maurauder bomber, 'Dinah-Mite'.

Why did Force U land in the 'wrong' place?
Most sources say Utah was so successful because Force U was 'mislanded'. However, a handful of demolition party boats led by an experienced officer, Lieutenant Commander Peterson, did land without loss on TARE GREEN Utah, the correct spot; demolitions proceeded,

25 Germans were captured and their pillbox was blown up – and without assault troops! Meanwhile, a combination of strong current and the absence of other Navy control boats led to the remainder of the force landing 2,200 yards away, halfway toward the Vire estuary. Nature also helped out, the storm tidal surge of 5 June which covered obstacles at H-Hour on Omaha allowing the LCVPs here to scud over the shallow, flat seabed of the Vire estuary and ride nearer to the high water mark before grounding just 700 yards short, rather than the 1,700 yards in normal conditions. German resistance was comparatively light.

See http://www.utah-beach.com
Source: *D-Day Then and Now,* ed. Winston G. Ramsey (After the Battle)

The American CG-4A Waco was a 48-ft long, 1.7-ton glider that could carry 13 troops plus pilot and co-pilot, who became soldiers upon landing. It was made of welded steel tubing and canvas with a honeycombed plywood floor to which a jeep or gun (but not both) could be strapped with nylon ropes or chains.

Only eight men, including General Pratt, were killed in the first night-time wave of 104 Waco gliders. There were many injuries however: 81 of the 375 men, or 22 per cent. The 140 used on D-Day by British forces were called Hadrians, and were crewed by Americans. The US forces used Horsas for their heavier material: 294 Wacos and 222 Horsas were despatched altogether behind the US sector of Utah.

Why were gliders used as well as paratroops?
Until seaborne forces could arrive, all vehicles, guns, ammunition, supplies and medical equipment in support of the paratroops could only be delivered by glider, to assigned LZs (Landing Zones). Less bulky loads could be dropped in cylindrical containers released from the bomb racks under aircraft wings. Gliderborne troops could be brought in in concentrations not possible for paratroopers, who would be dropped in 1,000 yard streams across the countryside and had to regroup, both men and equipment,

within their assigned DZs (Drop Zones) using 'crickets' (cheap toy clickers) and rattles in order to find each other in the dark.

Source: *Airborne Operations in WWII*, J.C. Warren (USAF Historical)

Above: D-Day: gliderborne troops pose for the camera.

The month of May had been the finest of the century. From 2 June the most complex series of depressions recorded in June in 50 years was proving difficult to interpret. Group Captain James Stagg had the job of presenting his assessment at the SHAEF HQ at Southwick House, near Portsmouth: the whole operation had to be postponed by 24 hours. Convoys had already set out and it was a tense moment while it was established that none had gone on alone and all had returned to port or to their moorings. Another day's delay would shift dead low tide forward an hour from the preferred timing and increase the risk of revealing the assault.

On 4 June, at the 2145 hour conference, Stagg announced a period of 'relatively good weather'. After conferring with his commanders, and with rain lashing the windows in a Force 8 storm, Ike said, 'Well, I am quite positive we must give the order ... I don't like it, but there it is, I don't see how we can possibly do anything else.'

At about 0415 hours on Monday the 5th the final decision was confirmed with the simple words, 'OK, we'll go!' The signal read, 'Halcyon plus 5 finally and definitely confirmed.' (Halcyon was the codeword for 1 June 1944.)

WHALE

This 200-ft long, 1,000-ton steel disembarkation platform was designed to slide up and down with the tide on four 90-ft high 'spuds' or legs planted on the sea bed. An electric winch controlled the operation and kept the platform rock steady, 6 inches above its natural free-floating position. It was connected to floating ancillary platforms which provided extra length and a turning space for vehicles. A line nearly a third of a mile long was set up opposite the village of Arromanches at the seaward end of the 1,200-ft roadways and connected these to shore. When constructed the platforms were the largest water-borne structures in Scotland, and the precursors of oil rigs. There were 22 planned and eight held in reserve. The term Whale also includes the roadway sections on floats, one piece of which was often already attached when the platform was being towed.

Pointe du Hoc is a 30 metre-high limestone promontory. The 2nd and 5th Ranger battalions, who were known as the Provisional Ranger Group (over a 1,000 men), were led by Lieutenant Colonel James Earl Rudder. Their mission was to destroy six 155mm guns set up in 1943 in open turntables behind the cliffs, half way between the future Utah and Omaha Beaches. They were also to eliminate a German observation post guiding shellfire from the promontory itself and cut off the coastal road between Omaha and Utah. The area was heavily bombed before, on and after D-Day, and shelled on D-Day itself and D-Day+1 – more than any other invasion site. The cratered landscape left by 3,264 bombs and shells weighing 1, 183 tons, as well as by Rangers' demolition, survives to this day and is preserved as an American Federal Memorial. Of the 450 men of 2nd Battalion who set out from England on 5 June, 77 were killed, 152 wounded and 38 missing; 5th Battalion losses were: 20 killed, 51 wounded and 2 missing.

See: www.abmc.gov
Source: *Rudder: From Leader to Legend,* Tom Hatfield, Texas A&M University Press

WHO NAMED THE BEACHES?

Omaha, Utah: Omaha and Utah were code names chosen for the First Army in March 1944 within General Bradley's London headquarters in Bryanston Square (near Hyde Park). Hitherto they had been referred to as 'X-Ray' and 'Yoke'. Gayle Ehler, from Omaha, Nebraska, a draftee and carpenter by trade (and building bunk beds in 1943) was assigned with a Class A pass to Bradley's HQ to convert the flat into a series of map rooms: walls had to be knocked through, plywood affixed. Another carpenter, named only as 'Sam', an Italian-American from Provo, Utah, worked with Eyler. The code names were Bradley's whimsical choice as a reward for their 'getting the place ready in double quick time'. On Eyler's death in 2003, his family found handwritten notes describing frequent informal chats with the 'GI General' over coffee, and this, after extensive investigation by the *Omaha World-Herald*, remains the best-attested theory.

The oft-repeated story that the two US beaches were named after the Corps commanders' home towns or states cannot be correct as Major-General Lawton Collins, VII Corps commander, was born in Algiers, Louisiana, and Major-General Gerow, V Corps commander, was born in Petersburg, Virginia.

Gold, Juno, Sword: David Belchem, Brigadier General Staff (Operations) for Overlord, chose the Second Army beach names from a standard army code-book as he planned the assault in detail with planning personnel who had already worked together in the plans for invading Sicily and Italy. His choice started out as GOLDFISH, JELLYFISH and SWORDFISH. However, JELLYFISH was already in use (see FISH). It was decided to remove the 'fish' – but this left the Canadians (who had lost more men in Operation JUBILEE in 1942 than the Americans would lose at Omaha in 1944 in a force one-sixth of the size) with an unhappy choice: JELLY. JUBILEE had already proved an unfortunate code name, given the result. The Canadians operated with code names beginning with 'J'; the matter was resolved by Wing Commander Michael Dawnay who worked on the Planning Staff, lodged (until April 1944) in the Marine Hotel in Troon, Scotland. He suggested the Canadians could keep the J by using his wife's Christian name, JUNO. The Planning Staff agreed: this rooted it in a robust and warlike mythical figure and also met the required syllabic clarity for radio links.

Source re Omaha, Utah: Henry J. Cortes OWH; Lt Col Hester Hansen on Bradley's HQ staff

See www.the-two-malcontents.com for the full story

Source re Gold, Juno, Sword: Patrick Dawnay; Brigadier David Belchem GSO Overlord Planning Staff, cited in *D-Day Then and Now*, ed. Winston G. Ramsey (After the Battle)

WINDOW

Packets of 5ft 6in-long strips of reflective tinfoil were dumped in the sea to create a radar picture in keeping with two spoof invasion fleets 6 miles long and 14 miles wide. It was also known as chaff. In Operation Taxable, Window was dropped from eight Lancasters of Leonard Cheshire's 617 Squadron heading for Le Havre. In Operation GLIMMER, six RAF Sterlings of 218 Squadron headed for Boulogne. Flying in the night of 5/6 June in a racetrack pattern about 8 miles long and 2 miles wide, at a speed of 180 m.p.h., their flight paths were methodically displaced in a south-easterly direction at a rate of 8 knots in order to mimic ships, all the time dropping Window. For added realism, Halifaxes fitted with Mandrel jammers accompanied the two 'fleets' but operated at low power to allow German radar to penetrate their ever-so-slightly ineffectual 'jamming'.

WOLKENKUCKUCKSHEIM
(CLOUD-CUCKOO LAND)

The Atlantic Wall was described by Rommel in November 1943 as a 'cloud-cuckoo land', and Normandy as 'a holiday camp'. He set about reinforcing the beach defences, laying 2.5 million mines by June. A total of 20 million were planned. Expecting a landing at high tide, he had placed many thousands of timber posts, tripod defences of angle iron and concrete tetrahedra on the beach flats. Many, but not all, were also mined. Areas at sea level were allowed to be flooded, notably the Vire and Dives estuaries. It was too little too late; 50 per cent of casemated positions were still under construction come D-Day and in the Cherbourg peninsula 85 per cent were without cover. Had he been appointed six months earlier the outcome of Overlord might have been different. As it was, no ship was sunk on D-Day by a shore battery so, despite his energetic supervision, his original assessment was proved right.

Created in January 1941 by Lieutenant Colonel T.A. 'Tar' Robertson, MI5's XX Committee held weekly meetings throughout the war to decide what information could be safely given over to the Germans, and through whom. The 40 agents in the 'Double-Cross' system each had a 'Case Officer' to check every word. By 1944 three quarters of all the work was to do with FORTITUDE, managing famous double agents like GARBO, BRUTUS and TRICYCLE. The latter, Dusko Popov (1912–81), was a wealthy Serbian philanderer and passionate Anglophile and was one of the inspirations behind James Bond. He accepted no payment from MI5, only from the Germans. His code name hinted at his penchant for 'threesomes' in his rooms in the Savoy. Both TRICYCLE and TATE (Wolf Schmidt) had their operations suspended for fear of 'blown cover', but after being provided with improved codes by their German handlers the assumption was correctly made that the *Abwehr* still trusted them. Both were therefore embedded in the FORTITUDE team and played key roles.

Y-STATIONS

Almost 8,000 stations around the world monitored enemy transmissions, both in clear and in code. A system known as 'Ping Pong' enabled sources to be pinned down to within a quarter of a degree, triangulation giving the exact location – hence the name Y-Stations. In a particularly devious trick, the RAF flew solitary reconnaissance missions on precisely defined tracks; the German reports on these missions were intercepted and decrypted, revealing locations of the radar stations that had tracked the aircraft. These could then be attacked with air-to-ground rockets which were fired from Hawker Typhoons.

Z: SEE PICCADILLY CIRCUS